District Gazetteers of India Series 11

ASSAM DISTRICT GAZETTEERS

THE SADIYA AND BALIPARA FRONTIER TRACT

District Gazetteers of India Series 11

ASSAM DISTRICT GAZETTEERS

THE SADIYA AND BALIPARA FRONTIER TRACT

B. C. ALLEN, C. S.

IN ELEVEN VOLUMES
(VOL. XI)

GYAN

Published by

Gyan Publishing House
5, Ansari Road
Daryaganj, New Delhi-110002
Phone: 011-47034999, 9811692060
E-mail: books@gyanbooks.com

Distribution Network
gyanbooks.com
India, USA, Canada, UK, Australia, France

ISBN: 978-81-212-8593-3 (Set) 11 Volumes
978-81-212-8582-7 (PB)
First Published, 1928

2nd Impression 2024

Printed at: Gyan Press, Delhi.

ASSAM DISTRICT GAZETTEERS THE SADIYA AND BALIPARA FRONTIER TRACT (VOL. XI)

Author: B. C. Allen

LIST OF VOLUMES

S. NO.	ISBN NO.	VOLUME	TITLE	AUTHOR	PRICE	PAGES
			ASSAM DISTRICT GAZETTEERS			
1	9788121285926	1st	Cachar	B. C. Allen	600	300
2	9788121285919	2nd	Sylhet	B. C. Allen	750	378
3	9788121285902	3rd	Goalpara	B. C. Allen	400	203
4	9788121285896	4th	Kamrup	B. C. Allen	675	344
5	9788121285889	5th	Darrang	B. C. Allen	725	364
6	9788121285872	6th	Nowgong	B. C. Allen	560	280
7	9788121285865	7th	Sibsagar	B. C. Allen	675	343
8	9788121285858	8th	Lakhimpur	B. C. Allen	690	347
9	9788121285841	9th	Naga Hills and Manipur	B. C. Allen	580	294
10	9788121285834	10th	The Khasi And Jaintia Hills, The Garo Hills And The Lushai Hills	B. C. Allen	675	363
11	9788121285827	11th	The Sadiya and Balipara Frontier Tract	B. C. Allen	375	190
			BENGAL DISTRICT GAZETTEERS			
12	9788121218672	1st	Angul	L. S. S. O'Malley	340	168
13	9788121259637	2nd	Bakarganj	J. C. JACK	970	194
14	9788121218696	3rd	Balasore	L. S. S. O'Malley	450	228
15	9788121259590	4th	Bankura	L. S. S. O'Malley	1000	199
16	9788121218375	5th	Bhagalpur	J. Byrne	390	194
17	9788121218290	6th	Birbhum	L. S. S. O'Malley	300	150
18	9788121259651	7th	Eastern Bengal and Assam - Bogra	J. N. Gupta	940	188
19	9788121218351	8th	Burdwan	J. C. K. Peterson	450	227
20	9788121259538	9th	Calcutta District Gazetteer - Statistics, 1901 - 02		340	68
21	9788121218313	10th	Champaran	L. S. S. O'Malley	410	205
22	9788121259613	11th	Eastern Bengal District Gazetters - Chittagong	L. S. S. O'Malley	1080	216
23	9788121259552	12th	Chota Nagpur Tributary		130	26
24	9788121259415	13th	The Cooch Behar Gazette: Statistics		1460	292
25	9788121218412	14th	Cuttack	L. S. S. O'Malley	490	248
26	9788121261357	15th	Eastern Bengal District Gazetteers Dacca	B. C. Allen	400	207
27	9788121218436	16th	Darbhanga	L. S. S. O'Malley	360	180
28	9789362089335	17th	Darjeeling	L. S. S. O'Malley	500	248
29	9788121259453	18th	Eastern Bengal District Gazetteers - Dinajpur	F. W. Strong	890	178
30	9788121259392	19th	Faridpur	L. S. S. O'Malley	700	140
31	9788121218474	20th	Gaya	L. S. S. O'Malley	540	270
32	9788121214032	21st	Bihar and Orissa District Gazetteer: Hazaribagh	E. Lister	715	234
33	9788121218337	22nd	Hooghly	L. S. S. O'Malley	680	340
34	9788121218191	23rd	Bengal District Gazetteer Howrah	L. S. S. O'Malley	390	199
35	9788121259293	24th	Eastern Bengal and Assam - Jalpaiguri	John F. Gruning	890	178
36	9788121259279	25th	Jessore	L. S. S. O'Malley	960	192
37	9788121259231	26th	Khulna	L. S. S. O'Malley	1100	220
38	9788121259217	27th	Malda	G. E. Lambourn	670	134
39	9788121267854	28th	Manbhum	H. Coupland	600	313
40	9788121218498	29th	Midnapore	L. S. S. O'Malley	500	252
41	9788121218597	30th	Monghyr	L. S. S. O'Malley	560	280
42	9788121259156	31st	Murshidabad	L. S. S. O'Malley	1250	250
43	9788121259576	32nd	Bengal District Gazetteers - Muzaffarpur	L. S. S. O'Malley	940	188
44	9788121259132	33rd	Mymensingh	F. A. Sachse	960	192
45	9788121259118	34th	Nadia	J. H. E. Garrett	1070	214
46	9788121259095	35th	Eastern Bengal and Assam - Noakhali	J. E. Webster	580	115
47	9788121218450	36th	Feudatory States of Orissa	L. E. B. Cobdenramsay	790	395
48	9788121259071	37th	Pabna	L. S. S. O'Malley	710	142
49	9788121218511	38th	Palamau	L. S. S. O'Malley	380	190
50	9788121218634	39th	Patna	L. S. S. O'Malley	500	250
51	9788121218535	40th	Puri	L. S. S. O'Malley	650	328
52	9788121218757	41st	Purnea	L. S. S. O'Malley	440	220
53	9788121258937	42nd	Rajshahi	L. S. S. O'Malley	1080	216
54	9788121256681	43rd	Bihar and Orissa District Gazetteers: Ranchi	M. G. Hallett	1350	278
55	9788121258913	44th	Eastern Bengal and assam - Rangpur	J. A. Vas	890	178
56	9788121218559	45th	Sambalpur	L. S. S. O'Malley	480	242
57	9788121214056	46th	Santal Parganas	L. S. S. O'Malley	940	308
58	9788121218610	47th	Saran	L. S. S. O'Malley	380	190
59	9788121218658	48th	Shahabad	L. S. S. O'Malley	380	190
60	9788121256704	49th	The Gazetteer of Sikhim	H. H. Risley	960	481
61	9788121218573	50th	Singhbhum, Saraikela And Kharsawan	L. S. S. O'Malley	560	280
62	9788121259439	51st	Eastern Bengal District Gazetteers - Tippera	J. E. Webster	730	146
63	9788121259033	52nd	24 Parganas	L. S. S. O'Malley	1420	284

S. NO.	ISBN NO.	VOLUME	TITLE	AUTHOR	PRICE	PAGES
			CENTRAL PROVINCES DISTRICT GAZETTEERS			
64	9789362081728	1st, Vol. A	Akola (Descriptive)	A. E. Nelson, C. Brown	870	436
65	9789362085481	2nd, Vol. A	Amraoti (Descriptive)	S. V. Fitzgerald, A. E. Nelson	1050	524
66	9789362089267	3rd,Vol. A	Balaghat (Descriptive)	R. V. RUSSELL	430	216
67	9789362083494	4th, Vol. A	Betul (Descriptive)	R. V. RUSSELL	610	306
68	9789362085146	5th, Vol. A	Bhandara (Descriptive)	R. V. RUSSELL	580	292
69	9789362088390	6th, Vol. A	Bilaspur (Descriptive)	R. V. RUSSELL	870	434
70	9789362086044	7th, Vol. A	Buldana (Descriptive)	A. E. Nelson	1090	543
71	9789362089014	8th, Vol. B	Chanda (Descriptive)	R. V. RUSSELL	470	234
72	9789362086938	9th	Chhattisgarch Feudatory State	E. A. De Brett	880	440
73	9789362082961	10th	Chhindwara (Descriptive)	R. V. RUSSELL	550	274
74	9789362089342	11th, Vol. A & B	Damoh (Descriptive and Statistical Tables 1891-1901)	R. V. RUSSELL	830	414
75	9789362081230	12th, Vol. A	Durg (Descriptive)	A. E. Nelson	460	232
76	9789362086037	13th, Vol. A	Hoshangabad (Descriptive)	R. V. RUSSELL	860	430
77	9789362086792	14th, Vol. A	Jubbulpore (Descriptive)	A. E. Nelson	950	474
78	9789362089663	15th, Vol. A & B	Mandla (Descriptive and Statistical Tables 1891-1901)	R. V. RUSSELL	370	186
79	9789362086419	16th, Vol. A	Nagpur (Descriptive)	R. V. RUSSELL	790	394
80	9789362080646	17th, Vol. A	Narsinghpur (Descriptive)	R. V. RUSSELL	510	257
81	9789362084835	18th, Vol. A	Nimar (Descriptive)	R. V. RUSSELL	600	299
82	9789362087737	19th, Vol. A	Raipur (Descriptive)	A. E. Nelson	790	396
83	9789362080264	20th, Vol. A	Saugor (Descriptive)	R. V. RUSSELL	570	285
84	9789362081117	21st, Vol. A	Seoni (Descriptive)	R. V. RUSSELL	460	232
85	9789362084965	22nd, Vol. A	Wardha (Descriptive)	R. V. RUSSELL	600	302
86	9789362083401	23rd, Vol. A	Yeotmal (Descriptive)	R. V. RUSSELL	550	277
87	9789362080325	24th, Vol. I, Pt. I	Gwalior (Text and Tables)	R. V. RUSSELL	980	489
88	9789362087133	24th, Vol. I, Pt. II	Gwalior (Maps)	R. V. RUSSELL	400	198
89	9789362086341	24th, Vol. I, Pt. III	Gwalior (Village List)	R. V. RUSSELL	810	406
90	9789362085467	24th, Vol. I, Pt. IV	Gwalior (Photos)	R. V. RUSSELL	1400	698
91	9789362087393	25th, Vol. II	Indore (Text and Tables)	C. E. Luard	1050	524
92	9789362084422	26th, Vol. III	Bhopal (Text and Tables)	C. E. Luard	540	272
93	9789362086815	27th, Vol. IV	Rewah (Text and Tables)	C. E. Luard	500	250
94	9789362087584	28th, Vol. V, Pt. A	Western States - Malwa (Text)	C. E. Luard	1520	762
95	9789362087300	29th, Vol. VI, Pt. A	Eastern States - Bundelkhand (Text)	C. E. Luard	930	463
96	9789362082169	30th, Vol. VI, Pt. B	Eastern States - Bundelkhand (Tables)	C. E. Luard	830	417
			GAZETTEER OF THE BOMBAY PRESIDENCY:			
97	9788121283441	1st, Part I	History of Gujarat	Ed.: James M. Campbell	3220	644
98	9788121285582	1st, Part II	History of the Konkan Dakhan and Southern Maratha Country	Ed.: James M. Campbell	4200	840
99	9788121285568	2nd	Gujarat, Surat and Broach	Ed.: James M. Campbell	2990	598
100	9788121285544	3rd	Kaira and Panch Mahals	Ed.: James M. Campbell	1690	339
101	9788121285520	4th	Ahmedabad	Ed.: James M. Campbell	1860	372
102	9788121285506	5th	Cutch, Palanpur, and Mahi Kantha	Ed.: James M. Campbell	2390	478
103	9788121285483	6th	Rewa Kantha, Narukot, Cambay, and Surat States	Ed.: James M. Campbell	1450	290
104	9788121285469	7th	Baroda	Ed.: James M. Campbell	3260	652
105	9788121285445	8th	Kathiawar	Ed.: James M. Campbell	3790	758
106	9788121285421	9th, Part I	Gujarat Population - Hindus	Ed.: James M. Campbell	3170	636
107	9788121285407	9th, Part II	Gujarat Population - Musalmans and Parsis	Ed.: James M. Campbell	1520	304
108	9788121285384	10th	Ratnagiri and Savantvadi	Ed.: James M. Campbell	2500	501
109	9788121285360	11th	Kolaba and Janjira	Ed.: James M. Campbell	2550	513
110	9788121285346	12th	Khandesh	Ed.: James M. Campbell	3190	638
111	9788121285322	13th Part I	Thana	Ed.: James M. Campbell	2050	413
112	9788121285308	13th Part II	Thana	Ed.: James M. Campbell	1770	357
113	9788121285285	14th	Thana - Places of Interest	Ed.: James M. Campbell	3290	659
114	9788121285261	15th Part I	Kanara	Ed.: James M. Campbell	2340	348
115	9788121285247	15th Part II	Kanara	Ed.: James M. Campbell	1740	348
116	9788121285223	16th	Nasik	Ed.: James M. Campbell	3490	698
117	9788121285209	17th	Ahmadnagar	Ed.: James M. Campbell	3860	772
118	9788121285186	18th Part I	Poona	Ed.: James M. Campbell	2930	586
119	9788121285162	18th Part II	Poona	Ed.: James M. Campbell	2680	537
120	9788121285148	18th Part III	Poona	Ed.: James M. Campbell	2500	503
121	9788121285124	19th	Satara	Ed.: James M. Campbell	3450	692
122	9788121285100	20th	Sholapur	Ed.: James M. Campbell	2730	547
123	9788121285087	21st	Gazetteer of the Bomaby Presidency: Belgaum	Ed.: James M. Campbell	2570	514
124	9788121285063	22nd	Dharwar	Ed.: James M. Campbell	4200	841
125	9788121285049	23rd	Gazetteer of the Bombay Presidency:Bijapur	Ed.: James M. Campbell	3550	712
126	9788121285025	24th	Kolhapur	Ed.: James M. Campbell	2250	450

S. NO.	ISBN NO.	VOLUME	TITLE	AUTHOR	PRICE	PAGES
127	9788121285001	25th	Botany	Ed.: James M. Campbell	2040	408
128	9788121284981	26th, Part I	Materials Towards a Statistical Account of the Town and Island of Bombay - History	Ed.: James M. Campbell	2500	504
129	9788121284967	26th, Part II	Materials Towards a Statistical Account of the Town and Island of Bombay - Trade and Fortifications	Ed.: James M. Campbell	2690	538
130	9788121284943	26th, Part III	Materials Towards a Statistical Account of the Town And Island of Bombay - Administration	Ed.: James M. Campbell	2450	702
131	9788121284929	27th	General Index	Ed.:R. E. Enthoven	2190	428
			MADRAS DISTRICT GAZETTEERS			
132	9788121258814	1st	Anantapur	W. Francis	1140	227
133	9788121258555	2nd	Malabar	C. A Innes & F. B Evans	3010	602
134	9788121258791	3rd	Bellary	W. Francis	1890	377
135	9788121258777	4th	Statistical Appendix For Chingleput		280	56
136	9788121258753	5th	Coimbatore	K. N. Krishnaswami Ayyar	3420	628
137	9788121232814	6th	Madras District Gazetteers District Gazetteer Cuddapah	C. F. Brackenbury	1120	285
138	9788121258715	7th	Statistical Appendix For Ganjam		370	73
139	9788121256766	8th, Vol. 1st	Godavari District Gazetteer	F. R. Hemingway	650	320
140	9788121256803	8th, Vol. 2nd	Godavari District Gazetteer	F. R. Hemingway	160	83
141	9788121258678	9th	Statistical Appendix For Kistna		640	127
142	9788121258654	10th	Statistical Appendix For Kurnool		270	54
143	9788121258616	11th	Madura	W. Francis	1900	379
144	9788121258579	12th	Statistical Appendix For Madura		740	148
145	9788121258630	13th	The Nilgiris	W. Francis	2190	437
146	9788121234276	14th	Madras District Gazetteers Gazetteer Of The Nellore District Brought Upto 1938		1150	386
147	9788121258517	15th	North Arcot		590	118
148	9788121258494	16th, Vol. 1, Part I	Salem	F. J. Richards	1710	343
149	9788121258593	16th, Vol. 1, Part II	Salem	F. J. Richards	1800	360
150	9788121258456	17th	South Arcot	W. Francis	2400	480
151	9788121258470	18th	Statistical Appendix For South Canara		400	80
152	9788121258432	19th, Vol. 1st & 2nd	Tanjore: Main Volume and Statistical Appendix		2070	401
153	9788121258395	20th	Tinnevelly	H. R. Pate	2740	547
154	9788121258418	21st	Statistical Appendix For Tinnevelly		320	64
155	9788121258371	22nd, 1st & 2nd	Trichinopoly: Main Volume and Statistical Appendix	F. R. Hemingway	2440	487
156	9788121241953	23rd	Vizagapatam District Gazetteer	W. Francis	760	385
			PUNJAB DISTRICT GAZETTEERS			
157	9788121255943	1st	Ambala District 1883-84		620	124
158	9788121255967	2nd	Amritsar		1180	236
159	9788121255981	3rd	Delhi		1300	260
160	9788121256001	4th	Ferozepore		950	188
161	9788121256025	5th	Faridkot		350	70
162	9788121256049	6th	Gujranwala 1893-94		1270	254
163	9788121256063	7th	Gujrat	C. E. Luard	1140	228
164	9788121256087	8th	Gurdaspur 1891-92		1260	252
165	9788121256100	9th	Gurgaon 1883-4		1020	203
166	9788121256124	10th	Hazara	H. D. Watson	2290	458
167	9788121256148	11th	Hissar district and Lohar State		1840	367
168	9788121256162	12th	Hoshiarpur		1420	283
169	9788121256186	13th	Jhang		1070	213
170	9788121256209	14th	Jhelam		1010	202
171	9788121256223	15th	Jalandhar District 1883-84		540	108
172	9788121256247	16th, Vol. XIV-A	Jullundur District, with maps and Kapurthala		1990	398
173	9788121256261	17th, Pt. I	Kangra (Proper)		1450	290
174	9788121256285	17th, Pt. II	Kangra (Kulu, Lahual, Spiti)		1800	357
175	9788121256308	18th	Karnal		1930	386
176	9788121256322	19th	Kohat		1540	307
177	9788121256346	20th	The Lahore District 1883-84		1220	244
178	9788121256384	21st	Ludhiana and Maler Kotla		1680	335
179	9788121256407	22nd	Lyallpur		735	147
180	9788121256421	23rd	Mianwali		1170	234
181	9788121256445	24th	Montgomery	P. J. Fagan	1590	318
182	9788121258364	25th	Multan (1901-02)	E. D. Maclagan	2400	480
183	9788121258708	26th	The Rohtak District 1883-84		980	196
184	9788121258746	27th, Vol. III A	Dujana State 1904		500	16
185	9788121256483	28th	Shahpur District		1780	356
186	9788121256506	29th	Simla District		800	159

S. NO.	ISBN NO.	VOLUME	TITLE	AUTHOR	PRICE	PAGES
187	9788121256520	30th	The Chamba State		2040	408
188	9788121256544	31st	The Chenab Colony 1904		1550	310
189	9788121256568	32nd	Kalsia State		270	53
190	9788121256582	33rd	Suket and Mandi		770	154
191	9788121256605	34th	Phulkian States, Patiala Jind And Nabha 1904		2070	414
192	9788121256643	35th	Simla Hill States		2220	443
193	9788121256667	36th	Sirmur		920	183
			RAJPUTANA DISTRICT GAZETTEERS			
194	9789362088994	1st, Vol. I-A & B	Ajmer-merwara (Text and Statistics Tables)	C. C. Watson	1230	246
195	9789362080882	2nd. Vol. II-A & B	Mewar Residency (Text and Statistics Tables)	K.D. Erskine	1700	339
196	9789362088444	3rd, Vol. III-A & B	The Western Rajputana States Residency And The Bikaner Agency	K.D. Erskine	3590	718
			UNITED PROVINCES OF AGRA AND OUDH DISTRICT GAZETTEERS			
197	9789362087560	Vol. I	Agra	H. R. Nevill	2260	452
198	9789362082466	Vol. II	Aligarh	H. R. Nevill	1300	260
199	9789362089779	Vol. III	Allahabad	H. R. Nevill	2050	409
200	9789362081346	Vol. IV	Almora	H. G. Walton	1670	333
201	9789362085658	Vol. V	Azamgarh	D. L. Drake Brockman	1750	349
202	9789362080547	Vol. VI	Bahraich	H. R. Nevill	1410	281
203	9789362085214	Vol. VII	Ballia	H. R. Nevill	1750	350
204	9789362084668	Vol. VIII	Banda	D. L. Drake Brockman	1750	349
205	9789362086518	Vol. IX	Bara Banki	H. R. Nevill	1720	344
206	9789362084101	Vol. X	Bareilly	H. R. Nevill	1640	327
207	9789362086631	Vol. XI	Basti	H. R. Nevill	1610	321
208	9789362083814	Vol. XII	Benares	H. R. Nevill	2290	458
209	9789362086105	Vol. XIII	Bijnor	H. R. Nevill	1820	363
210	9789362081674	Vol. XIV	Budaun	H. R. Nevill	1890	378
211	9789362086891	Vol. XV	Bulandshahr	H. R. Nevill	2100	419
212	9789362081520	Vol. XVI	Cawnpore	H. R. Nevill	2210	442
213	9789362088031	Vol. XVII	Dehra Dun	H. G. Walton	1710	342
214	9789362088710	Vol. XVIII	Etah	E. R. Neave	1600	320
215	9789362082992	Vol. XIX	Etawah	D. L. Drake Brockman	1390	277
216	9789362082220	Vol. XX	Farrukhabad	E. R. Neave	1620	324
217	9789362083869	Vol. XXI	Fatehpur	H. R. Nevill	1890	377
218	9789362085962	Vol. XXII	Fyzabad	H. R. Nevill	1700	339
219	9789362087997	Vol. XXIII	Garhwal	H. G. Walton	1270	254
220	9789362089892	Vol. XXIV	Ghazipur	H. R. Nevill	1600	320
221	9789362085436	Vol. XXV	Gonda	H. R. Nevill	1650	330
222	9789362080271	Vol. XXVI	Gorakhpur	H. R. Nevill	1890	378
223	9789362086129	Vol. XXVII	Hamirpur	D. L. Drake Brockman	1390	277
224	9789362087638	Vol. XXVIII	Hardoi	H. R. Nevill	1680	336
225	9789362081636	Vol. XXIX	Jalaun	D. L. Drake Brockman	1180	236
226	9789362084309	Vol. XXX	Jaunpur	H. R. Nevill	1750	350
227	9789362084187	Vol. XXXI	Jhansi	D. L. Drake Brockman	1960	391
228	9789362089168	Vol. XXXII	Kheri	H. R. Nevill	1650	330
229	9789362086778	Vol. XXXIII	Lucknow	H. R. Nevill	1760	352
230	9789362088635	Vol. XXXIV	Mainpuri	H. R. Nevill	1740	348
231	9789362080424	Vol. XXXV	Meerut	H. R. Nevill	2170	434
232	9789362081087	Vol. XXXVI	Mirzapur	D. L. Drake Brockman	2430	486
233	9789362085443	Vol. XXXVII	Moradabad	H. R. Nevill	1900	380
234	9789362082763	Vol. XXXVIII	Muttra	D. L. Drake Brockman	2140	428
235	9789362089915	Vol. XXXIX	Muzaffarnagar	H. R. Nevill	2260	451
236	9789362086143	Vol. XL	Naini Tal	H. R. Nevill	1890	377
237	9789362086761	Vol. XLI	Partabgarh	H. R. Nevill	1560	312
238	9789362081124	Vol. XLII	Pilibhit	H. R. Nevill	1570	314
239	9789362084453	Vol. XLIII	Rai Bareli	H. R. Nevill	1610	322
240	9789362088284	Vol. XLIV	Rampur	H. R. Nevill	1170	234
241	9789362083654	Vol. XLV	Saharanpur	H. R. Nevill	2190	438
242	9789362083142	Vol. XLVI	Shahjahanpur	H. R. Nevill	1510	302
243	9789362083623	Vol. XLVII	Sitapur	H. R. Nevill	1590	317
244	9789362089939	Vol. XLVIII	Sultanpur	H. R. Nevill	1330	266
245	9789362080851	Vol. XLIX	Unnao	H. R. Nevill	1530	305

ASSAM DISTRICT GAZETTEERS.

Volume XI.

SHILLONG :

PRINTED AT THE ASSAM SECRETARIAT PRESS.

1928.

Price Rs. 8-8.] [*Price* 13s.

Agents for the Sale of Books published by the Assam Government.

Agents in India.

(1) Messrs. Thacker, Spink & Co., Calcutta.

(2) Messrs. W. Newman & Co., Calcutta.

(3) Messrs. S. K. Lahiri & Co., Calcutta.

(4) Messrs. R. Cambray & Co., 6 and 8/2, Hastings Street, Calcutta.

(5) Babu Hari Ram Dhar, B.A., Popular Library, Dacca.

(6) Messrs. D. B. Taraporevala Sons & Co., 103, Meadow Street, Fort, Post Box No. 187, Bombay.

(7) The Indian School Supply Depôt, 309, Bow Bazar Street, Calcutta.

(8) Messrs. Rai M. C. Sarkar Bahadur & Sons, 90-2A, Harrison Road, Calcutta.

(9) Messrs. Students & Co., Cooch Behar.

(10) Messrs. Vas & Co., Madras.

(11) The Standard Literature Co., Ltd. 13-1 Old Court House Street Calcutta.

(12) The Standard Book Stall, Karachi.

(13) Messrs. Karsandas, Narandas & Sons of Surat.

(14) The Proprietor, New Kitapkhana, Poona.

(15) The Association Press, Calcutta.

(16) Messrs. Butterworth & Co., (India) Limited, Hasting Street, Calcutta, Post Box No. 2.

(17) The Director, The Book Company, Limited, Booksellers and Stationery, 4/4A, College Square, Calcutta.

(18) Kamala Agency, Shillong. (For List of Residents and Visitors to Shillong only.

ASSAM GOVERNMENT PUBLICATIONS ARE OBTAINABLE IN GREAT BRITAIN DIRECT FROM THE OFFICE OF THE HIGH COMMISSIONER FOR INDIA OR THROUGH ANY BOOK-SELLER.

SHILLONG:

PRINTED BY C. M. ROY, OFFG. SUPERINTENDENT, ASSAM GOVERNMENT PRESS.

THE SADIYA FRONTIER TRACT GAZETTEER.

PART I.

PREFACE.

The volume is to be read in continuation of Mr. B. C. Allen's Gazetteers of the Lakhimpur district, which supplies the history and description of this frontier area up to the year 1905. Since that time the Frontier Tract had become a distinct administrative unit, which renders desirable the issue of a separate Gazetteer.

NOTE—In connection with these notes reference must be made to the names of Rai Bahadur Lahman Chandra Hazarika '(Lahman Daroga)' and F. J. Needham, C.I.E., Indian Police, the pioner Political Officers of the Sadiya Frontier area, whose names have become legends and chronological marks in the tribal histories and stories. By his explorations and discoveries, Mr. Needham acquired and international reputatation and his work from 1882 to 1905 laid the foundations of the Modern North-East Frontier of Assam.

CONTENTS.

CHAPTER I.—PHYSICAL ASPECTS.

CHAPTER II.—HISTORY.

CHAPTER III.—ARCHÆOLOGY AND EARLY TRADITIONS.

CHAPTER IV.—POPULATION.

CHAPTER V.—TRADE AND INDUSTRY.

CHAPTER VI.—GENERAL ADMINISTRATION.

ASSAM DISTRICT GAZETTEERS.

CHAPTER I.

PHYSICAL ASPECTS.

Area and boundaries.

The Sadiya Frontier Tract is the North-East Frontier District of India, bordering on Tibet on the north and east and on Burma on the south and south-east. The District was formed in 1912 with headquarters at Sadiya and with the old Sadiya Subdivision of the Lakhimpur District as a nucleus, under the name "Central and Eastern Sections, North-East Frontier," which was later changed to the present designation. It lies between 27°15′ and 29° north latitude and 94° 15″ and 97° east longitude, extending from the Subansiri river on the west to the Lohit-Brahmaputra-Irrawady watershed. It includes the mountains on the southern face of the main Himalayan Divide, the western and north-western slopes of the Dapha and Phunkan ranges, which separate India from the extreme north of Burma and crosses the Patkoi Range to touch the northern end of the Hawkong Valley and run with the eastern portion of the unadministered area of the Naga Hills. Except where the district touches Lakhimpur, *i.e.*, on the south, its boundaries have not been demarcated, following mainly as they do the principal ridges of tumbled masses of mountains, which form the eastern extremity of the Himalayan system. The area of the Tract is some 10,000 square miles, of which 3,500 square miles are under regular administration. The latter area represents the plains and foot hills.

The boundaries officially notified are as follows :—

"From Siplumukh on the Subansiri east along the ridge of the outer range to the Jiya Dhol river ; thence down the right bank of the Jiya Dhol river to where it cuts the Rajgarh Ali ; thence east along the foot of the hills following the village path running along the foot of the hills so as to include all Galong villages to the Dipa (Sinyang) N., east-south-east of Dipa village ; thence down the right bank of the Dipa (Sinyang) N. to its confluence with the Simen river ; thence down

the right bank of the right channel of the Simen river to where it unites with the left channel to form one stream ; thence across and down the Simen (Dijmur) river to its confluence with the Burhi Suti ; thence east along the left bank of the Burhi Suti to the Sengajan road ; thence south-east along the Sengajan road to the Brahmaputra ; thence east along the right bank of the Brahmaputra so as to include Mesaki Chapari to the point where the Burhi Suti Channel takes off from the Brahmaputra river east of Pomua village ; thence across the Brahmaputra so as to include Dorkang and Kaplang Chaparis and along the Laika Jan to its common junction with the Mara Laika Jan and Ajuka N.; thence up the Ajuka N. to its junction with a small feeder stream connecting the Ajuka N. with the Dangori N. ; thence along the Dangori N. to its junction with the Dhola or Haokhati N. ; thence along the Dhola or Haokhati N. to a point (marked by a post, whence it runs southwards, marked '450' on the 1-inch to 1 mile map, the post being about one mile due west of Chhota Dirak village, which is situated on the Dirak Hka ; thence along the southern edge of the track running approximately eastwards to the Dirak Hka so as to exclude Chhota Dirak village ; thence south-east up the left bank of the Dirak Hka to where it is crossed by the village path from Mohanggaon to Bara Dumsa ; thence southwards along this path to Bara Dumsa and Bisa Pathar and along the western limit of Bisa Pathar and down the left bank of the Kolia or Koriapani (stream) to the Burhi Dibing or Namphuk river ; thence up the right bank of Burhi Dihing or Namphuk river to immediately opposite the Namchik confluence ; thence up the left bank of the Namchik river to the Namchik-Kathang Hka confluence ; thence up the Kathang Hka to the Kathang Hka-Lekha Hka confluence, thence up the Lekha Hka to its source at hill 894 ; thence down a small stream following a south-westerly direction to the Tirap river, thence up the Tirap river to its western source (Sumhak Ju) and the Patkai ridge ; thence eastwards (in conformity with the agreement between the Assam Government and the Government of Burma as to the interprovincial boundary)."

The general appearance of the District is that of mighty mountains overhanging tree-covered plain and of grassy expanse everywhere intersected—far west by large river beds and water courses which merge from stony submontane tracts into sandy alluvial plains covered with forest and gigantic grasses. The mountains are very steep and the rivers debouching from the higher levels splay over miles of country. The whole area is very sparsely populated with but little of the older alluvial soil which constitutes the wealth of Assam. Communications are mainly on the surface of the rivers or else hug their banks, and such villages as there are are confined to the neighbourhood of the main rivers. The sandy plains carry poor forest, the Simul tree (Bombax Malabaricum) being the main feature. On the higher levels evergreen forest prevails but the more valuable species are not found in profusion. General appearance.

The main artery of the province—the Brahmaputra river—enters Assam in the Sadiya District. Rising near the Monasorowar lake, away north of Kashmir it flows eastward as the Tsangpo through Tibet, being crossed by the India-Lhassa road at Chaksam ferry, not far from Lhassa and then turns southward cutting the main Himalayan axis at a point of which the approximate latitude is 29·35° and longtitude 95·20°. In its bend it encircles some magnificent peaks dominated by Namcha Barua (24,445′), at the northern foot of which lies, west and east, the gorge in which were supposed to exist the falls which remained a geographical mystery until 1913, when the area was explored by Captains Bailey and Morshead.* No falls were discovered but a series of rapids for thirty miles. The Tsangpo receives many tributaries in its course through the Abor Hills, the Ringong, Sirapateng (Sigong), Shimong, Siyom, Yamne and is known to the Abors as the Siang. It leaves the hills and enters the plains at Pasighat. A few miles Mountain and river system.

* The most detailed and reliable information available on the Tsangpo falls is that of the Ward-Cawdor Expedition, 1924-25, which visited, examined and mapped the course of the river through the gorge. Annexure C, page 95.

below Pasighat it divides into two channels—the Dihong channel and the Lalli—the island between, known as the Lalli Chapri, being a game reserve. Twenty miles south of Pasighat and west of Sadiya it is joined by the Lohit-Brahmaputra.

The Lohit rises in eastern Tibet where it is known as the Zayul and flows southward entering the district twenty-five miles south of Rima which is situated on the left bank. Thirty miles further south it turns due west at Minzang. In its course it receives many additions the Dou, Delei, Tidding, Digaru, Dibong, Kamlung, Noa Dehing and many smaller rivers which carry off the drainage of the huge mountain systems on both sides of its bed. The Lohit-Brahmaputra is known to the Mishmi tribes as the Tellu and in its journey through the hill section of the Frontier Tract flows through the Mishmi country and enters the plains at Parsuramkund, forty-six miles from Sadiya, a place of pilgrimage for Hindus.

The Dibong which joins it a short distance below Sadiya drains the mountain masses north of Sadiya and is notable for the deep gorges and inhospitable country of its upper reaches.

Feeder steamers can pass up the Brahmaputra at all seasons as far as Murkong Selek which lies 40 miles upstream from Dibrugarh, while from May to November they can penetrate a further fifty miles. As can be readily understood, the river is subject to big floods and at such times the junction between Sadiya and Kobo of the main stream and its two chief confluents, the Lohit and the Dibong, is a sight of savage relentless strength and beauty. The actual bed of the river is wide and in the cold weather it winds among huge sand banks or 'chapris' (islands of pure sand formed by the river and covered by grass or small tree jungle). The river is continually changing its course within its bed, eroding both banks in turn, this erosion has already destroyed one Sadiya and is even now a source of imminent danger to the existing town.

Communications in the plains are largely by river. All the important bazaars, Sadiya, Saikhoa, Kobo, Pasighat, Murkong Selek, are located on the Brahmaputra. The Assam Trunk Road (south bank) enters the District at mile 321, near Dholla village and reaches the Lohit-Brahmaputra at Saikhoaghat 324th mile and used to reappear on the north bank where formerly for 3½ miles it continued to Sadiya. Most of the north bank section of the Road has however disappeared into the river. Roads radiate from Sadiya. One goes north to Nizamghat (34 miles) running parallel and close to the Dibong river, *vid* Kirim, Bolung and Mishmi Bomjur villages. It serves as an outlet for the Dibong and Sissori villages and is passable for carts and light motor cars during the cold weather, November to May. A cart road runs to mile 21½ east where it bifurcates and thence (1) a cold weather cart road goes, *vid* Digarumukh (3½ miles) and Tizumukh (14½) to Temai (23½ miles) whence crossing the Lohit-Brahmaputra (Parsuramkund) is 4 miles by bridle track. (2) The second is the Lohit Valley road to Tidding river (77 miles), *vid* Payan (mile 36, cart road), and thereafter Tiki, Chikorpani, Denning, Dreyi and Theronliang, five stages by bridle track, each some 10 miles in length with furnished bungalows at each stage. Between Dreyi (5,200′) and Theronliang the road crosses the Tidding Saddle (6,000′) and drops 4,000 feet in 8 miles of bridle track. On a clear day a fine view of the plains is obtainable from Dreyi. The other main road in the District connects Kobo with Pasighat (21 miles) *vid* Pillung (11¾ miles), furnished inspection bungalows being found at all three places. This road continues as a bridle track into the Dihong Valley along the right bank of the river, *vid* Rengging (miles 18¾ on bridle track), Rotung (23 miles) to Yembung (33 miles) where Frontier outposts are stationed in the cold weather. About two miles from Yembung, on the left bank of the river is the memorial cairn to Dr. Gregorson who was treacherously murdered here by some Minyang Abors in March 1911. A similar cairn

Communications.

marks the actual spot where Mr. Nöel Williamson, Assistant Political Officer, whom Dr. Gregorson was accompanying, was similarly murdered at Komsing, 6 miles further on.

From Kobo a surface road leads to Murkong Selek (7 miles), where are found the Veneer Mills of the Assam Saw Mills and Timber Company. From Saikhoaghat railway station a surface cart road also leads to the vicinity of Rongdoi Miri village (12½ miles) on the left bank of the Brahmaputra immediately opposite Kobo, which is itself twenty-five miles down-stream from Sadiya.

Owing to the many large rivers the maintenance of through road communications is almost impossible. Saikhoaghat railway station, the terminus of the Dibru-Sadiya Railway which connects with the Assam-Bengal Railway at Tinsukia junction, is rail head for the Sadiya Frontier Tract. It is separated from Sadiya, the district headquarters, by six miles of the river bed of the Brahmaputra. The normal link of communication is the common dugout ferry of Assam, supplemented by the "*mar*" for vehicles, the time and track distance over sand depending on the state of the river. The ferry crossing on the north bank is at Parghat where the Assam Trunk Road, to which previous reference has been made, reappears three miles from Sadiya. Saikhoaghat is also rail head for Kobo and Murkong Selek.

Geology. Those interested in the geological formation of the Tract will find available information in the various Records and Memoirs of the Geological Survey of India and in Colonel Burrard and Sir Henry Hayden's account of the Himalayas. Through the kindness of the Assam Oil Company, a short account of the geology of the portions of the Sadiya Frontier Tract examined by the geologists is also available, and has been appended as an annexure to this volume.

The climate on the whole compares favourably with the rest of Assam, and Sadiya has a good reputation for health among Indians in general. There is a reasonable rainfall, and the snow-covered mountains visible from the river not only add to the natural beauty of the place but are the source of the melting snows which flood the rivers and soften the fierce heat of the summer season. There are, however, great variations in rainfall, very high figures being recorded at places close to the hills. Thus Pasighat averages some 200 inches yearly or double that of Sadiya. At places like Pasighat where the large rivers debouch on the plains, regular gorge winds occur nightly for months on end. Climate.

The Fauna is well varied, but no species occurs in any great number except possibly wild elephant, buffalo and tiger. Sambhur, hog deer and barking deer are found. The wild mythan is rare, as is also the swamp deer of Assam; in fact the existence of the latter was doubted until recently. The monkey tribe is strongly represented, the hoolook and other kinds being found on the hills as well as on the plains. The hoolook is sacred to some of the tribes who, as a rule, have few scruples as to their food. There is not a single specimen of the rhinoceros left, yet at one time both the Rhinoceros Indicus (the one horned Asiatic Rhinoceros) and another small kind were found, the latter possibly the Ceralorhinus Sumatrensis (small, two horned). All have been shot out by the tribesmen for their meat, hide and horn previous to our intimate administration. The domesticated mythan is very common among all the tribesmen and is the chief standard of wealth and barter. The Abors breed it largely for sale. That Zoological curiosity the 'takin' (Budorcas Taxicolor) is found in the Mishmi hills from 4,000 feet upwards. This animal is essentially a serow with affinities to the bovines through the musk ox and other relationships with the sheep goat and 'antelope' (J. Cockburn). The Binturong (Articurus Binturong) has been shot. The wild dog, the larger species, is not much in evidence. Small game birds are disappointing. Florican have practically Fauna.

disappeared, but the monaul and the blood pheasant are found in the distant hills. Partridge are practically non-existent and snipe are rare, but green pigeon afford good sport in the month of August. Geese and duck are met with in large numbers on the Brahmaputra and Dihong during their returning flight to Tibet and Central Asia. The rivers were famous for their mahseer but in the accessible areas the fish seem to have grown sophisticated. Wild elephant are fairly common and are a good source of revenue to Government, 123 being captured in 1922-23. Herds of wild buffalo are found near Sanpura which inter-breed with the village buffaloes let loose by the Khamtis, after the completion of the rice cultivation.

CHAPTER II.

HISTORY.

Introduction. The following résumé of the history of the hill tribes of the North-East Frontier and their relations to the British at Sadiya is in continuation of Chapters II and III of the Lakhimpur District Gazetteer in which an account of all frontier affairs up to the year 1905 will be found. It will perhaps enable the reader to understand more readily the great changes which have occurred since 1905, if we divide the twenty years now to be dealt with into three distinct periods. The first is that of Mr. Williamson's tenure of the post of Assistant Political Officer, Sadiya, under the old régimé. The second deals with the years of great activity on the North-East Frontier, consequent on Mr. Williamson's and Dr. Gregorson's murder by the Minyong Abors in March 1911. The third shows the progress of the new Frontier District, the formation of which was shewn to be necessary, as a result of the above-mentioned activities.

Mr. Williamson's period of office. As regards the first period, the success which marked Mr. Williamson's work at Sadiya may be summarised in the words used in the Political Report on the Abor expedition—" it opened a new era in our relations with the hills." In the course of a little more than five years the Assistant Political Officer, Sadiya, carried through a series of remarkable tours, all of which were most fruitful, both in establishing more friendly relations with the hill tribes and in increasing our knowledge of their idiosyncrasies and of the geography of the difficult country in which they live. It would be tedious here to recount all of these numerous tours, but a few of the more important should be mentioned. In December 1907 the Assistant Political Officer journeyed up the Lohit river as far as Sati, the last Miju village in the direction of Tibet. He travelled entirely on local transport and was everywhere received hospitably. In the same year he had toured through the foot hill villages lying between the Dibang river and the Simen river (Dijmur). In January and February 1908, a friendly visit was paid to Kebang, a Minyong Abor village lying three marches up the Dihong river from Pasighat, which had not been visited by a British officer since the disastrous expedition of 1858. In November and December of the same year, Mr. Williamson led a small expedition into the Rangpang Naga Hills to exact punishment from the village of Rashi which had raided the British Naga village of Wakpang in October 1907, killing seven British subjects. During this tour a considerable area of previously unknown country was roughly surveyed and a point reached from which the Hukawng Valley was clearly visible. In the cold weather of 1909-10, a second tour up the Lohit was made during which the Assistant Political Officer had an interesting meeting with the Tibetan officials of Rima.

Relations with the hill tribes.

Throughout this period our relations with the Taraon, Miju and Digaru Mishmis remained uniformly satisfactory. The Assistant Political Officer was materially assisted by the leading Khamti Chief, Chowna Gohain,* in his tours up the Lohit Valley, and the behaviour of the Khamtis and Singphos continued to be good. The Chulikata Mishmis also gave no trouble,

* Since deceased.

though with the exception of certain exempted villages, the tribe as a whole was blockaded as a punishment for their failure to capture the Bebejia Mishmi raiding gang led by Pongon Mideren of Elapoin. These savages had in 1905 killed three Dowaniya British subjects at Dikrang, a few miles from Sadiya, in revenge for Pongon's imprisonment during the 1900 Bebejia expedition. The Bebejias were blockaded throughout this period but none of the murderous gang was arrested.

Murder of Mr. Williamson and Dr. Gregorson.

Relations with the Padam Abors also continued satisfactory, but the conditions existing on the right bank of the Dihang river, where the Pasi-Minyong villages overlook the plains, caused the Assistant Political Officer considerable anxiety. The disquieting state of affairs on this section of the Frontier was not, to use Mr. Williamson's words, entirely the fault of the Pasi-Minyong Abors, and it was in order to establish our relations with those tribesmen on a firmer and more friendly footing that the Assistant Political Officer made many tours among these tribesmen, on the last of which he and most of his party were murdered at Komsing on March 31st, 1911. His companion Dr. Gregorson and some sick followers who had been left behind at Pangi village had been previously killed. It would be out of place to explore the very numerous contributing causes which led to this massacre, but the act which certainly precipitated it, was the murder, by men of Rotung village, of a Miri named Manpur and three sick coolies who had been sent back with letters by Mr. Williamson. This Miri boasted that his letters contained orders for the immediate despatch of troops to punish Rotung for the theft of some of Mr. Williamson's rations. The discovery of this theft had been made at Rotung by Mr. Williamson during his march to Komsing and for it Mr. Williamson had said he would require satisfaction on his return. The hot-heads at Rotung immediately determined that the Miri should never reach the plains with the letters and, in accordance with this resolve, all four men were murdered near Renging next morning.

By this murder, the party hostile to Mr. Williamson, already strong, was considerably augmented and, urged on by the argument that, as punitive measures were certain to be attempted by the British for the murder of the Miri and the coolies, it was obviously the wisest course to slaughter all intruders who could give information either of the country or the events leading up to the massacre, the Kebang and Rotung men crossed the Dihang and killed all Mr. Williamson's party, except 6 coolies who managed to effect their escape.

The second of the three periods is thus reached.

The murder of Mr. Williamson naturally caused great excitement along the Frontier and many of our subjects living near the Pasi-Minyong border showed signs of panic, which however was allayed by the prompt measures taken by the Deputy Commissioner, Lakhimpur, and the Commandant of the Military Police Battalion stationed at Dibrugarh. A force at once advanced to Pasighat, but no general advance was possible to Kebang and Komsing owing to the lateness of the season. A stockade however was erected at Balek, a Pasi Abor village situated five miles from Pasighat, and commanding this group of five Pasi villages, and several expeditions against hostile Minyong villages were carried out successfully. The activities of this force effectually protected the Frontier from raids by the Abors till the Abor expedition was mobilized and commenced its operations late in 1911. It had been decided that, on this occasion, no risks were to be run in dealing with Rotung, Kebang and the other Minyong villages which were implicated in the massacre, and an exceedingly strong force under the command of Major General Bower was despatched to execute the orders of the Government of India. These orders were :— Operations on the Frontier.

(1) To exact severe punishment and reparation for the murder of Mr. Williamson and Dr. Gregorson and their party.

(2) To visit as many Minyong villages as possible, and make the tribe clearly understand that in future they would be under our control, which, subject to good behaviour on their part, would be of a loose political nature.

(3) To visit the Padam village of Damro.

(4). To explore and survey as much of the country as possible, visiting the Pemakoi falls, if practicable, and incidentally settle the question of the identity of the Tsangpo and Brahmaputra rivers.

(5) To submit proposals for a suitable frontier line between India and Tibet.

The opportunity was also taken to despatch three missions, up the Lohit, into the Miri country lying to the west of Subansiri river, and up the Dibong river, in order that the work done, in the matter of the instructions conveyed in items (4) and (5) above should be part of a comprehensive whole, and not merely an isolated achievement on a section of the Frontier. It was hoped that as a result of these combined operations a complete and much-needed survey would be effected of the tumbled mass of inhospitable mountains which stretch from the plains of Assam to the main range of the Himalayas, the natural boundary of Tibet and Assam.

Results of the expeditions.

Though the full results which were hoped for when these orders issued were not realized, very valuable work was done during the cold weather of 1911-12. The actual operations and achievements of the Abor expedition are matters of public knowledge and it is sufficient to say that the expedition established our military superiority in the estimation of the Abor tribes generally and the Minyongs in particular, that it confirmed the friendliness of the Padams, whose chief village Damro, was visited, and that it accomplished much useful survey and exploration work. Simultaneously, the three missions mentioned above achieved considerable success in surveying and bringing into closer touch the areas with which they were called upon to deal. At the end of the working season, it was decided not to leave all this valuable work unfinished and accordingly late in 1912 the Abor survey commenced its operations. Linked with this, another survey party was despatched to complete the mapping of the area drained by the Dibong river and its tributaries, surely some of the steepest country that exists. Two of the officers who accompanied this party crossed the Dibong-Dihang divide, in the vicinity of the main Himalayan range, to the Upper Dihong valley and continued their explorations into Tibet. Thence they emerged into the Darrang district of Assam many months later, after a most adventurous journey which solved finally those much discussed geographical questions, the existence of the Tsangpo falls and the identity of that river with the Dihong of Assam. The Abor survey party on their side succeeded in crossing the Doshung-La pass and reaching Phea Doshung on the Tibet side of the main Himalayan range. On the return of these two parties, it was found that the desired survey had, with the exception of one or two unimportant areas, been completed throughout the mountains drained by the Dibong river and by the Dihong in its course south of the main range. Meanwhile, further east, the Walong promenade had visited Rima in Tibet, and the Mishmi work party and the Public Works Department had commenced the construction of the Lohit Valley Road from Sadiya with a view to the opening up of communications in that direction. Another interesting tour was made during the cold weather of 1912-13 by an Assistant Political Officer through the country to the south of the Lohit stretching as far as the Turong river to the south and the Noa Dehing to the east. During this tour all the Singpho and Khampti country and so much of the Rangpang Naga country as fell within the proposed boundaries of the new North-East Frontier district was visited, and friendly relations established throughout.

Peace and progress.

With the conclusion of these operations our second period comes to a close and we may proceed to review the quiet advance effected since the establishment in 1914 of the North-East Frontier district as an administrative unit separate from the regulation district of Lakhimpur. This administrative change was found essential in order to continue the closer relations with the hill tribes which the activities described above had brought about. These operations had naturally established our prestige firmly among the wild frontier tribes, and thus rendered possible during ensuring years a period of peaceful and almost uninterrupted progress. During the operations of the Abor expedition and of the Mishmi and Miri missions, it was decided that for the future the numerous hill tribes who border the plains of Assam from Bhutan in the west along the ranges of the Himalaya to the Mishmi country of the Lohit Valley, together with those south of the Lohit who inhabit the plains and western slope of the Patkoi, should be dealt with by Political Officers working directly under the orders of the Government of Assam. Previously they had been controlled by the Deputy Commissioners of Darrang and Lakhimpur, but events had proved that these officers had already more than sufficient work in carrying on the ordinary administrative duties of their districts and had little time to spare for touring among, and thus becoming acquainted with, the hill tribes who overlooked them.

Administrative changes.

Accordingly the North-East Frontier was divided into three sections, the Central and Eastern Sections to control the Rangpang Nagas (excluding those of the Lakhimpur Frontier Tract), the Singphos, Khamtis, Miju, Digaru. Chulikata and Bebejia Mishmis and the various tribes of Abors as far as the Simen-Subansiri divide, and the Western Section to deal with the tribes from this divide westward to Bhutan. With the latter we are not here concerned, but the two North-East Sections were placed in the charge of one Political Officer with headquarters at Sadiya, the name being subsequently changed to the more simple " Sadiya

Frontier Tract." One Assistant to the Political Officer was placed in charge of the Abor subdivision with headquarters at Pasighat. A Lohit Valley subdivision with headquarters at Walong was also at one time mooted, but owing to the continued good behaviour of the Lohit Valley Mishmis and the civilising effect of the Lohit Valley road, this project was found to be unnecessary.

To impress on all tribes the fact of our sovereignty over the plains, all villages whether Galong, Pasi, Minyong or Padam Abor, Chulikata or Digaru Mishmi, Khamtis or Singphos, cultivating in the plains were assessed to poll-tax and after a little opposition on the part of the Padam villages, which broke down when it was found that the demand was made in earnest, this poll-tax has since been collected without trouble through the agency of the village "gams." Buying or selling of slaves has been prohibited in all the villages under our control, while the cultivation of the poppy which had been common before our administration of the foot-hill villages has been put down with a severe hand.

The only incidents which call for remark during the period are those in connection with the Bebejia Mishmis. It will be remembered that this tribe had been blockaded up to the time of Mr. Williamson's murder, on account of Pongon Mideren's raid on Duanias at Dikrang in 1905. After the survey operations up the Dibong Valley in 1912, during which Pongon's arrest was not effected, it was decided to abandon the blockade, and, assisted by settled conditions and a new policy of selling by auction all hill produce for the benefit of the hill men, subject to a deduction of ten per cent. for auction tolls, the trade in hill commodities increased rapidly. Chulikata and Bebejia Mishmis visited Sadiya in increasing numbers, attracted by the improved prices their 'teeta' and musk obtained. Thus in 1917 Tagi Mideren, one of the Dikrang murderers, was arrested in Sadiya and subsequently hanged. In revenge for this, three Mideren of Elapoin murdered

Recent incidents.

with poisoned arrows a rifleman of the Assam Rifles, only a few hundred yards away from the Nizamghat Post.

Owing to the European War and other causes it was not until 1920 that the punishment of this savage village was undertaken, but though tardy it was severe, for Pongon was shot while attempting to ambush the column, and Elapoin village was destroyed.

CHAPTER III.

ARCHÆOLOGY AND TRADITIONS.

Early history.

To render intelligible an account of the ruins and remains to be found within the Sadiya Frontier Tract, it is necessary first to give a brief outline of the early history of its inhabitants so far as this is known. There are no records or traditions available prior to the advent of Chutiyas whose Buranji gives the first recorded mention of Sadiya. The Chutiyas are believed to have been members of the great Bodo race, to have come from the north-east, and to have lived in large independent communities like the Nagas and Abors of the present day. There is a tradition, however, that the Chutiyas originally came down the Subansiri valley, and that one Bibar, a local chief, attained a measure of supremacy over the other villages. This position was improved by his son, who called himself 'Lord of the Hills' and descended the Brahmaputra valley, where he defeated Bhadra Sen and founded a capital at Ratnapura on the Majuli, or in North Lakhimpur. Gaur was at that time under Hindu dynasty, so the Chutiya eruption must have been previous to 1204A.D. The Chutiya leader, assumed the name of Ratnadwaj Pal, excavated tanks, constructed forts, etc., and there are to-day within seven miles of modern Sadiya large tanks with bricked sides which are believed to have been originally excavated by the Chutiyas. The remains of forts at the foot of the hills, at Bishemnagar and at other places, are probably traceable to the same times. Ratmadwaj is said to have visited Gaur and on his return left a son there to be educated. The boy died and the body was sent back to the father, who received it when he was building a new city. This he called in memory of the event—'Sadiya' (the place where the corpse was given).

The Ahom records show that when they entered Assam in 1228 A.D. the Chutiyas were established at Sadiya and were masters of the country westwards as far as the Disang river. Hostilities broke out about the middle of the 14th century, and in 1523 (or according to the Chutiya chronicles about 1673 A. D.) the Ahoms finally defeated the Chutiyas at Chantam or Chandangiri.

There are said to have been four subdivisions among the Chutiyas, namely, Hindu, Ahom, Deori and Borahi. The Deoris are the old priestly caste, attendants on the gods, and possibly the class from whom the annual sacrifice was at one time chosen. Their original home was on the banks of the Kundil but, harried by the hill tribesman, on the decline of the Ahom Raj, they moved westward. Their temples are said to be copies in wood and thatch of the famous copper temple at Sadiya, which was at one time a centre of worship for all the tribes. The Deoris.

The chief gods are three:—(1) Gerasi Geri (Bura buri) worshipped by the Debongia Khel, (2) Phisadema (Bolia Hemata) or elder son, worshipped by the Tengapaniya Khel and (3) Peshasi (daughter), who is known as Tameswari Mai (mother of the copper temple) and also as Kechakhati (eater of raw flesh), the latter name being given in memory of the annual human sacrifice, formerly offered to the goddess and provided by the Ahoms until Gouri Nath Singh's time. The particular class from whom the victims were taken were said to have been in existence in Sadiya in Hannay's time (1846-47). Deities.

It is thought by some that the Ahoms introduced human sacrifices and that Hindu, Buddhism and Bramanical Buddhism existed from the earliest times and absorbed the Shans (Ahoms). They hold that the influx of tribes about the middle of the 15th century caused a reversion to anarchy and barbarism, a possible cause of the downfall being schisms between the followers of Siva and Vaisnava, and, that to these schisms and not to the Shan invasion, are due all the ruins and unfinished remains above mentioned. A revival of Brahminical Hinduism with the introduction of Brahmins from Gaur finally absorbed (about 1611-49 A. D.) the Tai (Shans) who had previously absorbed the 12 Rajs (Bara Bhooyans).

Architectural remains.

Whatever the facts of the origin of Sadiya there are at least many remains pointing to a former importance. On the Deopani and Debong rivers, and probably the Kundil also, are many tanks, some as big as six acres in area, perfect oblongs with bricked sides and ghats. Perhaps the most interesting of these relics is what is known as the Sadiya Stone Pillar. This is octagonal in shape, eleven feet in height on a base fifteen inches square, with a vase capital and serpent entwined thereon, with raised carvings and all sculptured from a single block of stone. It was found lying in the jungle close to the seventh mile post on the eastern side of the road from Sadiya to Nizamghat, adjoining some squared stones which formed part of a small bridge leading to the ghat of a large brick-sided tank. The pillar bears an inscription in the Ahom language, and cannot be earlier than the first quarter of the 15th century, when Sadiya first came into the hands of the Ahoms: the probability is that it is of a much later period. The substance of the inscription is as follows:—

"I, the Dihingia Bargohain, do engrave on the stone pillar and the copper plate these writings (with the strength of which) the Misimis are to dwell on the hills near the Dibong river with their females, children, attendants and followers. They will occupy all the hills. They will give four basketful of poison and other things as tribute and keep watch on the body of the fat Gohain (Sadiya Khowa Gohain). If anybody happens to be in possession of and wishes to remain on all sides (of the hills), he is prohibited from encroachment. If anybody would dwell by the side of the hills, he would surely become a slave (of the Misimis).

I do proclaim wide if anybody sits exalted (*i.e.*, comes in power, *i.e.*, becomes ruler) he should not break (the agreement) and break the stone."

The Mishmis still occupy the area mentioned, *i.e.*, the neighbourhood of Nizamghat, and this fact would point to the date of the pillar being late in the period of the Ahom government of Sadiya. The poison was probably one of the poisonous aconites which are still in common use for hunting and medicine. The pillar has been removed to Sadiya and erected on the maidan.

Again at Bishemnagar or Bishmuknagar, situated near Chipulin village up the Balijan (Sanpura) river and accessible from mile 27 on the Lohit Valley road, is the remains of a large fort and settlement. It is supposed to have been built by Raja Bishmook or Bhikrum, Raja of Kundilpur, father of Rukmini.

The following 'thans' or shrines are also in existence: that of Buraburi in Bazalgaon village, of Bolia Bhaba in Moria, of Keshakati or Tamesweri in Lakhimpuria village, of Patarhal in Kokaramara and finally of Dehingthan in Dokangaon. The last named is venerated by the Nadiyal caste. Shrines.

The shrines were primarily Chutiya places of worship, and the priests were Deoris as is the case now, but there are also Ahom 'pujaris' and the shrines are objects of veneration to all Hindus, and semi-Hindus. The most important nowadays is Bolia Baba Than which is but a name, there being no buildings of any kind, and it is a common form of settlement in local disputes and cases for the parties to adjourn there to take oaths. The solemn affirmation of the courts is far less efficient than Bolia Baba in ensuring the telling of the truth. There are also *nahor* trees to be found on the neighbourhood of the tanks, which tree is planted by Buddhists.

Lying up the Ghurmura river beyond Borgaon, there is said to be another shrine named Bura Buri which tradition tells us was the most ancient and holy spot in Upper Assam and the place from which all other objects of worship sprung.

The Copper Temple.

Another notable ruin is the Tameswari Mai, or so-called Copper Temple, situated on the right bank of a small stream, the Dol or Dewûlpanee of the Assamese of Hannay's days, 8 miles east of Sunpura, within a mile of mile 27½ of the Lohit Valley Road. It is said that the worship was of Yoni, or of the Linga of Siva in conjunction with Yoni, and that human sacrifices were made. Hannay who visited it in the season of 1844 described it as follows "Interior 8 feet square, walls 4½ feet thick, exept in front; 2 recesses on each side of the door which was formed by 3 entire blocks of stone of massive size—the lintel being a roughly squared block 12′ × 2′ 3″ × 16″; walls quite plain inside and out except lintel and sides of door way". The roof was said to be covered with sheets of beaten copper. The two Linga were in the middle of a large stone inside. Hannay considered that the building he saw was a reconstruction, owing to the presence of 'surki' (Journal of the Asiatic Society of Bengal, June 1848.)

Lieutenant Dalton also described the place as follows:—

"A small stone square building, nearly square, built without cement, the stones being joined by iron pins not clamped, the roof was of copper: the interior is 8 feet square the whole being enclosed by a brick wall 130′ × 200′ near the west wall is a small stone tripod for human sacrifices—victim provided by Ahom Rajas latterly probably malefactors condemned to death but formerly of a particular khel of the Rajas subjects who had to provide one and who had privileges on that account and were known as 'Sarh' or free. Victim had to be of pure caste and perfect form—even the boring of an ear rendered them unfit. Brahmins were excluded as a privilege. Doms, Haris, Musulmans and women as unfit. Six hundred victims supposed to have been offered up in all in the course of 6 centuries. Lasted till the subversion of the Ahoms by the Burmese ".

Buchanan's 'Eastern Kamykya' stated that 'Tamese-serimai' was situated on the Dikkori Basini near north eastern boundary of ancient Kamarupa situated on the 'Dol or Deoûl Panee.' Before the Shan or Ahom invasion eastern Kamarupa was accessible to western India by a raised road from Cooch Behar to the eastern confines of the Assam Valley. When the Ahoms adopted Hinduism, though western India was shut off, a road ran from Sadiya *viâ* Sanpura to Tameseri. The Sadiya Khowa Gohain is said to have lived at Sanpura. The Rajgarh Ali which is still in existence from Tezpur, *viâ* North Lakhimpur appears in sections as far east as Diphu, nine miles east of Sadiya. The Rajgarh Ali though jungle covered is a well defined feature from the Subansiri river due east to the Jiyadhal river. Then it disappears, though here and there at the foot of the hills near the Sisi river and to the west of Pasighat stray bricks are found. As a road the Rajgarh Ali appears again between the Gaurmara river and the Kundil near Diphu staging camp, where it forms a forest reserve boundary, crosses the Kundil, and continues to the Diphu river near Sengsap Khamti village. The Rajgarh Ali.

Near the Dobang village of Luru on the Gogar stream, about one mile above its confluence with the Sisi, there are not inconsiderable remains of old shrines made of carved sandstone, which have collapsed. The idol is a work of some merit, as are the Lingum stones and the beds in which they are set up. The shrine is known to the Dobang Abors as 'Matri Malanti' and is respected by them. The Dobang ruins.

Some 28 miles beyond the site of the Tameswari Mai, along the pilgrim cart road which proceeds *viâ* Digarumukh, Tezumukh and Temeimukh where the Lohit is crossed, one reaches Parsuramkund, where the Lohit-Brahmaputra river emerges from the hills. This is a sacred place of pilgrimage for all Hindus and is Parsuramkund.

visited yearly by some thousands. There are said to be the remains of a tank and buildings in the forest along the right hand of the Lohit between Tezu and Temei. The Lohit emerges through a magnificent defile and forms a backwater or pool in the rocks. On the left bank is the sacred pool of the Kund, which consists of large masses of rock strewn in every direction. The following account of the traditions of Parsuramkund is available through the kindness of a Brahmin gentleman, and is inserted as being of considerable interest.

"In ancient times Santonu Rishi with his wife Amogha devoted themselves to life long worship of the Supreme Being living on the bank of Manas-Sarowar (western Tibet). After a long time Brahma being pleased with their prayer appeared personally before Amogha while Santonu was away performing his ablutions in the Manas-Sarowar lake and offered to bless her with a son (Putrabar). Amogha, frightened at the sudden appearance of a four-headed being, took him to be a demon and closed the door of her cottage. She related this to Santonu on his return. Santonu regretted the foolishness of his wife (in refusing the blessing of Brahma) and, after examination of the spot where Brahma stood, found something glittering on the earth. It was Brahmabirja (seed of Brahma). Santonu swallowed the Brahma-Birja himself and in due course became pregnant—Brahma took pity on the Rishi who as a result gave birth to the river Lohit (lit.—red water) which collected in a pool at the spot where it was discharged. Santonu blessed Lohit with the assurance that one of his descendants would set him free from that place. After a long time Jamadagni's son Parsuram who killed his mother by order of his father with an axe visited all the sacred places and shrines as atonement for his sin, but the axe by which he killed his mother stuck to his hand and would not fall off. Being instructed by Brahma he went to a 'Brahmin' named Bishnujosha who advised him to go to the lake where Lohit was detained. Parsuram did so, bathed in the lake and the axe fell from his hand. Now Parsuram thinking of the supreme value of the water of the pool determined to make the water accessible to all men, so that the sinners of all kinds might make atonement by bathing in the holy water. He accordingly cut an outlet and thus allowed the water to take its own course towards the inhabited areas. But as soon as he arrived at the spot now known as Brahmakunda, Lohit found him (Parsuram) quite tired, took pity on him, appeared in person and instructed him to go ahead. He (Lohit) himself followed him. The outlet cut by Parsuram is still visible and tepid water flows from the same."

CHAPTER IV.

POPULATION.

The following is a brief account of the various tribes who are found in the Districts, and may be read in conjunction with the interesting description given in Chapter III of Mr. Allen's Gazetteer of the Lakhimpur district. Introduction.

The Miris living in the plains are a riverain people dwelling on the Brahmaputra and its tributaries, and call themselves Mishing, 'Miri' being the Assamese word for 'go between, or interpreter.' The Miris who live downstream from Dibrugarh in Lakhimpur, and on or near the Majuli in Sibsagar, are known as Chutiya Miris, possibly indicating a claim for connection with the one time rulers of Upper Assam. They seem a much more settled prosperous, virile, Hinduised type than their upstream brethren, living east and north-east of Dibrugarh and mostly in the Sadiya Frontier Tract, who have traditions of arrival in Assam, *vid* the Subansiri and Dihong Valleys. The Dihong is the Siang of the Abors and the Tsangpo of Tibet. These Miris call themselves 'Siangiya' as opposed to 'Chutiya' and were driven southwards by the more virile Abors from the north, who had been forced over the main Himalayan divide by various Tibetan tribes of whom the Pemakoibas now The Miris.

occupy the Dihong Valley north of the Abors, in the vicinity of the place where the Tsangpo makes its great turn from east to south to flow towards Assam.

The Pemakoibas have a fair degree of civilisation and despise the Abors as savages: the latter in turn have always looked down on the Miris as slaves.

In the Sadiya Frontier Tract the Miris live in small communities, inhabiting *chang* houses, and practising *jhum* cultivation under primitive conditions. Their women folk are industrious. Their communities are enlarged by the arrival of runaways usually of the slave class from Abor villages. The language of the Miris and Abors is identical, pointing to a possibility of their being originally a servile section of the Abors, and many of them speak Assamese. Until our intimate administration of the North-East Frontier was undertaken, they had been always used by the former Assamese Government and ourselves as the channel of communication with the Abors, and to them may be traced not a few of our former misunderstandings with the hill men. They are good boatmen somewhat addicted to opium and are gradually becoming more Hinduised. The total number of Miris in Assam is 68,725, of whom the majority live in Sibsagar, Lakhimpur and the Sadiya Frontier Tract.

The Abors. The word Abor in Assamese means unknown or 'savage.' The Abor tribes occupy the area lying between the Subansiri and the Dibong rivers, and at the last census of 1921 numbered very nearly 12,000. They are divided into endogamous tribes. Of these the Dobang or Galong live between the Subansiri and the Sidho (Dikari) rivers, in small communities who are inclined to move periodically, and have some customs of a polyandrous origin. Some have settled in the plains, where their physical deterioration is apparent and they have taken to the opium habit. The Dobang were once distinguished by the number of their slaves. The position of the better classes of women folk among them is good, the marriage price being very high and the wife having a clearly defined position of authority. Their cultivation is similar to that of the other tribesmen. They work as cane cutters and to a certain extent at felling and logging timber. They are animists in religion.

Next, are the Minyang, living eastward of the Dobangs and extending up to the Dihong river. Their main area is the Dihong Valley. An offshoot, the Pasi-Minyang, who formerly occupied the Yamne Valley, now live in a group of villages close to Pasighat the headquarters of the subdivision. Many of the Minyang, and all the Pasis dwelling in the foot hills and the plains, pay poll-tax.

The Padam—the 'Bor Abor' of Frontier history—occupy the area between the Dihong and Dibong rivers and with the exception of the parent village Damorh and a few villages in the Yamne Valley all dwell in the foot hills and plains and are ordinary poll-tax paying rayats. Since our occupation of Assam, several operations were undertaken against the Minyang and Padam. None of the earlier were strikingly successful and consequently the Minyang and Padam, naturally blusterers, continued to hold an exaggerated opinion of their own power and a corresponding contempt for our administration, which culminated in 1911 in the treacherous massacre by the Minyang of Mr. Williamson, Assistant Political Officer, Sadiya, Dr. Gregorson, who was accompanying him, and their 42 followers and coolies. Mr. Williamson had visited some Minyang villages in 1909, and was again visiting them in 1911 at the invitation of some of the leading men of Riu village when he was treacherously attacked at Komsing, Dr. Gregorson having been massacred the previous day. The Military expedition sent to exact reparation for the murders, brought home to the Abors the power and resources of Government, and since then their country has been surveyed and explored and a loose political control established over their hills. Both the Minyang and Padam live in large communities, and some villages even contain 400 houses. They are an intensely democratic people, among whom the institution of slavery still survives, and all freemen have—and usually exercise—a free voice in the 'Kebang' or village council to which everything, however trifling, is referred and there discussed at inordinate length. The Kebang is nominally presided over by the gams or headmen whose positions depend solely on their personality, force of character or wealth, and on the following they can gain thereby for themselves. The Padam and the Minyang Abors are essentially men of words, who become great heroes if they see their bluff is succeeding. They are well administered in their own primitive way. The taking of human life is very rare amongst themselves, though with a lead they would go to great extremes, given the opportunity and absence of opposition. Though a state of 'war' is not uncommon between villages, the opposite sides rarely meet and operations usually consist of negotiations and threats conducted through third parties. They respond to firm, just administration. Their political unit is the village rather than the tribe or clan, though offshoot villages will look up to a parent village while not altogether or always acknowledging its authority. They live in 'chang' houses and 'jhum' extensively. Their women folk, who lead a life of child bearing drudgery, and the children are industrious. Their actual fighting qualities are not conspicuous though in 'Kebang' they are desperate fellows. They are good bridge builders, some tubular cane bridges over the Dihong river being more than 500′ in length. Their crops are rice, maize and millet, the last named being mainly grown for the manufacture of 'apong,' a mild beer, of which they drink quantities. They do not appear to be addicted to opium though they cultivate it to some extent, mainly for medicinal purposes. Their main wealth is in domesticated mythan, which they breed and trade. Their arms are the sword—bought from Tibet—and the long bow and poisoned arrow. Their only iron tool and instrument for all purposes is the *dao*. Both Padam and Minyang are animists. All Abors are monogamous as a rule. They are at first sight a sullen, exclusive, unlikeable people full of their own importance, men of words rather than deeds living in an extremely mountainous country with an excessive rainfall, which causes dense jungle and semi-tropical vegetation to flourish right up to the permanent snow level. With more intimate intercourse with them one laughs at and with them and ends by liking them.

In the Valleys of the Sisseri, and Dibong rivers and of their tributaries are found the people known among themselves as the Midu and Mithun and to the Assamese as the Chulikatas (crop-haired) and Bebejiyas. It may be mentioned that the Padam and Minyang Abors crop their hair in similar fashion to the Chulikatas. There are no practical differences between the Bebejiya and the Chulikata whose languages, habits and customs are identical and who intermarry. They are a very primitive sturdy people, living in villages which rarely exceed 20 houses, in what is perhaps the poorest, wildest and most precipitous country in India traversed by rivers with gradients of unusual steepness the result of torrential rains. They have barely progressed beyond the development of the family unit. As opposed to the stay-at-home Abor, all the Mishmi tribes are great travellers about their own country. There is no cohesion among them, nor any particular tribal institution, unless it be the prosecution of feuds. If a Mishmi is wronged or considers he is wronged his Mishmi 'law', as he calls it, compels him to exact punishment with his own hand and, as a rule, this punishment consists in stealing a mythan or killing or seizing for ransom some relative or connection or slave of the offending party, the latter being naturally very much on the alert if he knows there are grounds for a quarrel. As relatives and connections are bound in tribal honour to avenge themselves for such killings, there are some long standing vendettas in existence. Each village is completely independent of its neighbour but feuds are not unknown within the village. Headmen are only so in name, the heir starts off with an advantage but he must maintain it by his character or wealth and ability in village council. Their arms are the sword, long bow and poisoned arrow.

The Chulikata and Bebejiya Mishmis.

Their cultivation is *jhum*; all seeds are sown on the same plot and each crop is reaped as it ripens. The *dao* is their only implement, and their crops, the usual maize, millets, cotton, tobacco and rice. In their hills is found the 'teeta' root, a rhizome of which the active principle is berberine and which they collect and sell at Sadiya. The musk deer is found in the higher valleys, and musk pods are also obtained by barter from the Tibetans and sold at Sadiya. Some villages have settled in the plains and pay poll-tax. They are not a very numerous people but their wild fierce appearance and rude manner, and the reputation of the country in which they live, have ever made them the terror of the plainsman. Isolated instances of attacks on individuals and villages are on record and the tribes have at times being blockaded. It is not improbable that at one time the Chulikata and Bebejiya were shot at sight by the plainsman when the latter had the advantage, and that their raids were affairs of tribal honour. They are active traders in 'teeta', musk and domesticated mythan which they buy from the Abors. They are animists and monogamous, a very primitive people, men of deeds as well as words, with the ordinary virtues and failings of human nature.

The Taroan or Digaru Mishmis.

East and south-east of the Bebejiyas and inhabiting the north bank of the Lohit Valley and of its tributaries from the north up to and including the Delei river are the Taroan or Digaru Mishmis, a quiet people, at the western end of whose area is the sacred pool of the Brahmakund where the Lohit-Brahmaputra emerges from the Hills, a place of pilgrimage for Hindus. They trade with Sadiya and live in villages of a few houses, but each house shelters many. A man's wealth is gauged by the number of his wives. They are addicted to the opium habit and are under loose political control. Their weapon is the cross-bow, a Tibetan sword being usually carried for ornament.

The Miju Mishmis.

East of the Taroan, occupying the Lohit Valley from the Delei river and the whole of the south bank of the Lohit Valley from the Brahmakund, are the

Miju Mishmis known among themselves as the M'ju. They are a quiet people, physically superior to the Taroan, with whom they occasionally intermarry, and are opium consumers. Like all other tribes in the Sadiya Frontier Tract their main trade is with Sadiya, they barter their purchases with the Tibetans of Zayul and occasionally of Rima, which is the most prominent village in south-eastern Zayul on the Lohit river (Tibetan Zayul Chu). They are polygamists, and animists in religion.

The Khamtis.

Hunter's Statistical Account of Assam, Volume I gives a detailed account of the Khamtis as they were but unfortunately are no longer All Khamtis west of the Burma divide, *i e*, in Assam, are now ordinary poll-tax paying rayats except their one Chief Raja Chowna Numshaum of Choukham on the Te'eng river Sadiya Frontier Tract, whose clan have been temporarily exempted. They are a likeable, comparatively advanced people with their own language written in the Burmese script, professing Buddhism. But they are also an opium sodden people and a dying race, as their numbers show. All the Khamtis in Assam were enumerated in 1921. Of the total number (2,958), 1,460 were in the Sadiya Frontier Tract. Most of the remainder are settled in Lakhimpur, but a few live in the Balipara Frontier Tract and Sibsagar. Efforts are being made to wean them from the opium habits by the restriction of sales of opium to registered consumers only, a measure admirable in intention if not strikingly effective in practice. They live in some twenty small villages varying from a few houses to over 50 in the head village of Choukham, and in some cases are intermixed with Singphoes. The Khamtis too, have lost most of the enterprise and virility described by Hunter. Chowna Raja, since deceased, is the only chief among them, he is now very old and with his death will disappear the only Khamti who possesses outstanding ability and influence, particularly in relation to the Mishmis who hitherto have always looked up to the Khamtis.

Nagas, Sadiya Frontier Tract.

The regular administration of some of these tribes and clans was undertaken from 1923-24. Previous to this, enquiries into thefts by Nagas of iron rails from the collieries in the vicinity of Ledo brought to light the fact that the practice of human sacrifices undoubtedly still obtained among the Rangpang clans south of the Patkoi range. The Rangpang clans living on the northern slopes of the Patkoi, whilst admitting that they had made them in the past, denied that there had been any in the present generation. These latter Rangpangs were forthwith brought under direct administration, assessed to house-tax and the survey of the area taken in hand and will be completed in 1926. This has brought the regularly administered area of the district to the crest of the Patkoi Ridge looking down on the area where barbarism still survives and to eradicate which the Governments of Assam and Burma are co-operating.

The detailed information available at present is given herewith :—

Habitat.

The Nagas occupy the hills in the eastern portion of the southern area of the Sadiya Frontier Tract between the plains of Assam and Burma and may be conveniently divided into (1) those between the plains area of the district and the Patkoi Ridge, *i.e.*, Cis-Patkoi, (2) those between the Main Patkoi Ridge and the Assam-Burma boundary—Trans-Patkoi. Actually between the Patkoi Ridge, the upper Chindwin district of Burma, the Hukawng Valley on the east and the Naga Hills district of Assam on the west is practically an unexplored area, inhabited by Rangpang and other Nagas. Those living in the hills adjoining the Hukawng Valley are to some extent under the influence of the Sesan Singpho (Chingpaw) Headmen of Shinbwiyang, etc., living in the Hukawng Valley.

The Cis-Patkoi tribes of the Sadiya Frontier Tract consist of— Cis-Patkoi.

(1) Laju (Laiyu) and Hatut clans: 16 villages, 1,125 houses, 11,200 souls, living in the head waters area of the Tirap river in an area of about one hundred square miles, *i.e.*, a density of over 100 to the square mile a fact which will in time become an administrative problem owing to land hunger. These two clans are not administered.

(*ii*) The Moklum: 6 villages, 185 houses, 1,300 souls who may be classed with the Laju and Hatut; the Yogli and Rangrang both Rangpang clans, who live in ten small villages, 800 people, living between the Tirap river and the Namchik-Tirap watershed.

(*iii*) The Longri, Moshang, Longphi, Rongrang, Tulem—all Rangpang clans; Yungkup, Kamlau and Tikkak—30 small villages—2,000 people in the Namchik River Basin and Eastwards. (*ii*) and (*iii*) are all administered from Sadiya, though at present administration consists only in cold weather tours and the collection of a house-tax of Rs. 2 per house. Sadiya to them has hitherto been but a name.

The noticeable features about the Laju and Hatut are the comparatively large village communities. Laju the main village of the clan, consisting of some 400 houses with a population close on 4,000 is, however, exceptional. These two clans with the Moklum seem to have affinities with the Namsang and other clans of the south-west and west and have probably been forced northwards along the western slope of the Patkoi by the clans of the Mokokchang unadministered area. They do not keep slaves and deny performing human sacrifices. They are head hunters and the skulls are preserved in the 'morungs' or meeting houses. Laju, has a good collection, Borduria a small village (60 houses), in the Lakhimpur unadministered Naga area, is in proud possession of a collection of many generations, several hundred skulls being carefully preserved and arranged in the 'morung'. The headmen are elected and their influence rests largely on individual character and personality. The men are physically well-developed but slight in build, averaging 5' 3" and the elder men often refined and slightly aquiline in appearance though the younger men are coarse and heavy looking. They shave the front of the head but allow the rest of the hair to grow wearing it gathered up in a knot at the back of the head. The high pointed narrow hat of closely woven cane decorated with pigs' tushes and bristles and toucan (hornbill) feathers is common and with this and pierced ears ornamented with serow horns or flowers or porcelain beads—the young 'buck' is a pleasing sight. The Laju women clip their hair as close as possible. Both clans are polygamous. The Laju bury their dead while the Hatut burn. Each village has its young men's 'club' or clubs each with its 'canoe' drum twenty feet in length and two feet in diameter. When beaten alternately in unison by ten or twelve men ranged on either side the effect is impressive and the sound travels a great distance and messages broadcasted. There have been no inter-clan raids of recent years. The arms are the broad bladed *dao* and spear and an occasional flint lock gun, and effective shields of bark are used. The Laju, unlike the Hatut and all the others, do not come down to work in the plains. The former are the middlemen—astride the trade route—between the Nagas to the west from whom they take salt, and trade opium, *daos* and spear-heads from the Trans-Patkoi Nagas to the east.

Borduria in Lakhimpur unadministered area has twenty brine wells and supply salt as far away as the Hukawng Valley. To the west of the Laju, between them and the Sibsagar Naga area, live the Nivong, who are said to go naked and are despised accordingly. Even the children of the Sadiya area people wear clothes. Both men and women tatoo—the men from the shoulders to the solar plexus a V shaped diagram on chest and back in lines half an inch apart as well as serrated lines round the neck when they have taken a head and the women the lower part of the forehead and upper part of the nose. Slaves are not kept. Very many of the men and some of the women smoke opium.

They are prosperous, contented and healthy—they can more than hold their own in their area and treasure their independence and do not want to be interferred with by administration or otherwise. The Laju people have been credited with supplying, *i.e.*, selling victims for human sacrifice to the Rangpang clans. They deny it. It is very probable that they did so in their old raiding days.

As regards (*iii*) who live north-east of the Moklum, they are, with the exception of the Tikkak, Kamlau and Yungkup Rangpang clans who have migrated in search of food and land over the Patkoi from the basin of the Dilli (Namphuk) river where their parent clans and affinities still live. They are in physique and general virility inferior to the Laju, Hatut and Moklum.

There is but little known at present of these Naga tribes and clans. The Hukawng Valley is a historic route of invasion of India from the south-east and these Nagas are possibly early arrivals, pushed aside by the Ahom and Kachin tides of movement, having been left behind by some pre-historic conquerors of Assam. It is noteworthy that other peoples of Assam History are believed to have been addicted to human sacrifice, *i.e.*, Chutiyas, the Ahoms, Cacharis, Kochs, etc.

The Rangpang clans are monogamous and some burn and some bury their dead. They are addicted to opium which is grown everywhere in the Trans-Patkoi area. They keep to themselves and there is but little inter-clan trade. Though their language is one there are noticeable difference in dialect between the clans.

All Nagas do '*jhum*' cultivation, rice and *kochu* (arum tuber) being the staple crops. They keep cattle, buffalo, pigs and fowls. The monotony of their primitive lives is varied by feasts which are held on the slightest pretext.

Trans-Patkai Nagas.

The main area of the Rangpang clans is the basin of the Dilli (Namphuk Hka) river system which is a tributary of the Chindwin river. To the east is the Kachin—settled Hukawng Valley, while on the west are the big raiding Naga villages in the unexplored area east of the unadministered area of the Naga Hills district of Assam. The clans are Moshang, Morang, Langshing, Yogli, Sangke, Shangwa, Mimung, Katsan, Longri, Longphai, Sograng, Sangtai, Dungai, Motai, Tulim, etc. The general description already given of the Rangpang of the administered area cover them—a people in no way impressive, living in unkempt hamlets.

Human Sacrifice.

This custom has been and is a normal practice among all Rangpang clans who explain it as a reaction to felt necessity to appease the spirits. It is primarily a personal or communal votive and intercessionary gift and will be vowed in times of difficulty, *i.e.*, promised for the future if a victim be not immediately available and it is such promises already made to the spirits, which many clans in the unadministered area have advanced as one of their main reasons for not immediately abandoning the practice, *i.e.*, the fear of retribution due to the non-fulfilment of such vows. More than one household may subscribe to purchase a victim : in time of urgency a slave victim may be borrowed to be replaced later or may be bought on credit and even buffaloes, etc., stolen to provide part of the price. Victims who are generally slaves, captives in war, may be of either sex and any age and cost from Rs. 300 to Rs. 500. Doubtless, useless members of the community are seized and sold and also weak, helpless debtors in a powerful turbulent village. Rangpangs do not supply any victims themselves and all admit that the source of supply is away to the south and south-west, *i.e.*, the Dilli (Namphuk) river basin and westwards, *i.e.*, west of the Sandri Bum and Magri Bum Ridges where Rangpang area may run with the big raiding, head hunting Naga villages in the unexplored area east of the Assam-Burma boundary in the unadministered area of the Naga Hills district of Assam. The Rangpang not only sacrifice but traffic in victims, the Dilli basin people not only buying from the west and sacrificing but buying and reselling; in fact it is probably the custom for a victim to pass through more than one hand before meeting his or her end. The slaves are always described of being of an unknown clan, tattooed on the cheeks and forehead and speaking an unknown tongue. The Rangpang of the administered area give the Laju clan as one of the sources of supply in the past. The Laju dwell just inside the Sadiya Frontier Tract unadministered area—in the most northerly of the big head hunting villages and though they deny keeping slaves or trafficking in them, it is extremely probable that some of them did in the past. They number some 7,500 people. When purchased for sacrifice, the victim is kept in the house of the owner, well cared for and fed but kept in stocks if there is any suspicion that escape may be attempted. The sacrifice is within a month of purchase unless bought for resale. On the appointed day, selected, as is the executioner, by divination by the 'wise' men, the victim is drugged with opium or drink or, failing these, even beaten into insensibility, led to the front of the front verandah of the house and decapitated by a blow or blows on the neck from behind at the top of the notched tree which serves as a ladder entrance to the verandah. The skull when clean is divided in two perpendicularly and the front hung suspended in the verandah room. As for the body, one account is that the body is divided up and the bones, flesh and entrails are sold as charms or divided among clansmen. Another account is that the body is buried in the jungle and when the bones are cleaned they are distributed or sold. Others have stated that the body is buried unmutilated. The executioner, it may be noted, is never of the household of the donor of the victim.

It has often been alleged that runaway coolies from the Assam tea gardens, and coal mines, earthworks, etc., have been enticed away by the Rangpang and others, seized and sold as victims: enquiries have hitherto failed to elicit any evidence whatsoever to support these allegations.

The march of time and progress has brought Government to the question of eradication of this horrible custom. The preliminary enquiries have disclosed a problem of real magnitude. The area concerned inhabited by those who sacrifice and those who are the source consists of tumbled masses of mountains inaccessible and practically all unexplored, totalling in area at least 10,000 square miles. The intimate administration of this area is at present beyond practicability. The obvious action for immediate suspension is the cutting off of the source of supply of victims. Even were Government in an easy position to enforce by arms immediate orders to abandon the practice—which it is not, something more than a force is required. At first sight it is easy to assert that with people who have not emerged from barbarism the only law until such time as they can be educated to a higher state of reasoning and conduct is force. Here are children of nature, isolated, hitherto working out their own destinies with social customs, primarily the result of physical environment. Analysis of the principles of human action, which explain particular events in this matter as in everything else must be made and the results studied. Government have started to make it clear beyond all possible doubt and compromise that the practice is opposed to all humanity and these ideas becoming widely prevalent are a substantial coercion to right-thinking according to civilisation. Travelling back in thought to the background of our own history in which

Sun-worship and Druidical rites are a dim memory, one can approach the question with understanding and a spirit of patience and of hope and this spirit will give vision and initiate a reasoned onward movement from barbarism. There will be advances and relapses but progress will continue. A good number of villages have already publicly undertaken to give up the practice so there is in existence a right-thinking section to show the way to their fellows. As little interference as possible and full liberty to arrange the personal details of their lives compatible with our ideas must be the policy. Enthusiasm with patience is necessary if pressure and success is to result, looking beyond the immediate effect of what actual action is taken. So much for theory and generalisation, there remains the details of immediate effort indicated. These peoples must be systematically visited by sympathetic understanding officers from Burma and Assam from the south and east and from the north and west respectively and regular campaign undertaken on the lines indicated. Where reasonably possible main routes and inter-village tracks must be improved to become Belloc's 'channels, not only of trade but of ideas and of progress, to move and control them intellectually as well as physically.'

These notes are the results of hurried tours on the fringe of the Rangpang country and it is hoped that they will serve as a basis for the preparation of detailed reliable information of these peoples.

Those who desire further information about the various Frontier Tribes will find much that is instructive and interesting in Captain Michell's Report on the North-East Frontier of India, published in 1883, and in Hunter's Statistical Account of Assam, Volume I, issued a few years earlier. Mr. B. C. Allen's Gazetteer of the Lakhimpur district, 1905, has already been mentioned as containing an interesting description of these peoples. Earlier counts.

CHAPTER V.

TRADE AND INDUSTRY.

The principal mart is Sadiya, the headquarters of the district with a population of 2,300, situated on the north bank of the Lohit-Brahmaputra at the Kundil river confluence. Rail head is six miles away, at Saikhoaghat on the Dibru-Sadiya Railway, whence the journey to Calcutta *viâ* Tinsukia junction, Lumding and Amingaon takes forty-five hours. Communication with Saikhoaghat across the Brahmaputra, which is here 1¼ miles broad and consists of a sandy waste through which the river wanders, is by the usual antiquated dugout ferry. In the rainy season from May to November, Sadiya is occasionally served by a weekly feeder Steamer Service from Dibrugarh. In the dry season the feeder cannot ply above Murkong Selek the headquarters of the Assam Saw Mills and Timber Company, Limited. Trade.

Practically all trade is in the hands of the Marwari community the only people in the district possessing capital, enterprise and business instincts. The local inhabitant, whose wants are few and who is usually an opium consumer, suffers from a mental paralysis, the result of climate and environment. At any rate, he prefers the indolent ease of his shady house to the turmoil and to him distressing energy necessary in business of any kind. Had he his way he would continue to hypothecate his growing, or even unsown crops to the Marwari shop-keeper to meet the pressing financial demands of the moment, paying enormous percentages for short-term loans. This pledging and orrowing has now been forbidden by executive order.

The Sadiya bazar during the cold weather months teems with primitive and often extremely dirty hillmen who come down to sell their produce, or in the case of the Digaru and Miju Mishmis to work at jungle clearing, cane cutting, etc. With the development of Upper Burma and the Hkamtilong and the opening up of the Hukawng Valley from the southern end, the Khamtis and Kachins of the area south of the Dapha range are not often seen in Sadiya nowadays.

Imports and exports.

The chief imports are cloths, yarn, salt, utensils and agricultural implements. The exports in addition to the hill produce of 'teeta,' musk and wax are *gur* and potatoes and Abor rugs (gadus). The sale-totals of the past eight years show that the tribesmen's imports of hill produce average well over Rs. 50,000 a year of which probably not more than twenty per cent. is spent in local purchases, the balance being expended on the purchase of domesticated mythan for festive occasions or else re-invested for further trade in hill produce, since the actual vendor is more often than not a middleman and not the actual collector. Hill produce is sold in public auction over which the Political Officer presides and payments are personally made by him to the vendors to secure them a fair price. Ten per cent. of all prices realised is paid by the vendors and credited to the Sadiya Local Fund.

Markets.

The Sadiya Local Fund is in a prosperous financial condition owning its own markets and bazars at Sadiya, Saikhoa and Pasighat. The threat of erosion to Sadiya town and headquarters is however an ever present anxiety and the actual site of Sadiya market is seriously threatened. Sadiya is a daily market, while those at Saikhoaghat and Pasighat are held twice weekly.

Minerals and jungle products.

Hitherto no coal or oil has been found, though there are indications of both in the south-eastern area of the district, which is adjacent to the rich coal and oil areas of Ledo and Digboi. Limestone is available in large quantities in the river beds close to the foothills, and is not too inaccessible to be worked in big quantities

The forests are full of good cane, the sole right to cut which brings in an annual revenue of some Rs. 15,000, while thatching grass produces Rs. 12,000 yearly. The true *Chaulmugra* tree (Tarakto Genos Curzii, and not the Gynocardia) is found, and its fruit yields the genuine *Chaulmugra* oil which is known as a specific for cutaneous diseases. This oil has come into great prominence recently owing to its efficacy in Sir Leonard Roger's treatment of leprosy. Another chief export of the district is forest timber in the form of tea boxes, etc. The Assam Saw Mills and Timber Company, Limited, have a veneer Mills at Murkong Selek and a tea box Mill at Leimekuri. *Goor* and potatoes are exported in fair quantities. Practically every other commodity is imported, including rice, the local surplus being negligible. A small amount of paddy is exported.

Musk pods, wax and Mishmi "teeta" are brought in by the tribesmen, to the total value of some Rs. 70,000 yearly, between the months of November and February inclusive and are sold by the Political Officer and his Assistants in open auction ; all finds its way to the Calcutta market. Mishmi teeta (teeta Coptes) is of two qualities, the thick variety being the superior and having just double the value of the thin. It is found wild and is cultivated in the Mishmi hills by the tribesmen. The Dibong Valley supply being found and cultivated at high altitudes is all first class, the Lohit and its subsidiary valleys supplying the second quality. The first class fetches nowadays Rs. 500 to Rs. 600 per maund and is brought for export to China, *viâ* Calcutta. It is a small stemless herb with perennial root stock met with in the temperate regions of the Mishmi hills of Assam. The plants are said to grow on the ground among the moss around the stems of trees. Its uses, etc., are described at length in " the Commercial Products of India" (Watt). The supplies available yearly in the Sadiya market are some 100 maunds of first class teeta, 40 maunds of second class, 70 to 80 maunds of wax and 400 tolas of musk.

Fisheries.

There are five mahals on the rivers which are let yearly for a small sum. The Nadiyals or hereditary local fishermen caste, of whom there are four small villages, all tend to resort to agriculture. This tendency combined with want of enterprise makes the supply of fish hardly equal to the small local demand.

CHAPTER VI.

GENERAL ADMINISTRATION.

System.

The administration is in charge of a Political Officer and two Assistant Political Officers, usually seconded from the Imperial Indian Police, and law and order are maintained under the Frontier Regulations. Administration is of a firm patriarchal character under which the tribesmen are, as far as is consistent with justice, made to administer their own personal affairs under the guidance of the Political Officer. Sadiya is the headquarters of the district. There is one subdivision, Pasighat, with headquarters at that place in charge of an Assistant Political Officer, comprising the area between the Dibong river and the western boundary of the Tract. Sadiya itself is also the headquarters of a Civil Surgeon, a Forest Officer and an Executive Engineer.

Criminal and Civil Justice.

Special rules are in force for the administration of criminal justice in the Sadiya Frontier Tract, and are as follows :—

1. The administration of the Sadiya Frontier Tract is vested in the Governor of Assam, the Political Officer and his Assistants and the native village-authorities.

The Political Officer shall nominate and appoint the village authorities, subject to the confirmation of the Governor of Assam and shall assign to them their respective functions under these rules, and define, so far as may be necessary, the local limits within which such duties shall be exercised by each, respectively, and may cancel and modify any such order. When no village authorities have been so nominated and appointed, the powers and duties assigned to them by these rules shall be exercised and performed by the Political Officer or by such other officer as he may depute for this purpose.

2. The ordinary duties of the Police in respect of crime will be discharged by the village authorities. They shall arrest all criminals and maintain peace and order within their respective local limits.

3. An appeal shall lie from all orders of the chief village authority in Police matter to the Assistant Political Officers, and from them to the Political Officer, whose orders are final, but the Governor of Assam may at any time call for the proceedings, and modify or reverse any order of the Political Officer.

4. Criminal justice is ordinarily administered by the Political Officer and his Assistants. The Political Officer is competent to pass sentence of death, transportation or imprisonment up to the maximum amount provided for the offence, of whipping, and of fine up to any amount. Provided that all sentences of death or transportation and all sentences of imprisonment of 7 years and upwards shall be subject to the confirmation of the Governor.

5. The Governor or Political Officer may call for the proceedings of any officer subordinate to him and reduce, enhance or cancel any sentence passed, or remand the case for retrial.

6. An appeal shall lie from the decision of an Assistant Political Officer to the Political Officer. No appeal shall lie as a matter of right from any sentence passed by the Political Officer involving less than 3 years' imprisonment. An appeal shall lie to the Governor against sentences of 3 years' imprisonment and upwards, and from all sentences of death or transportation. The jurisdiction of the High Court of Fort William at Calcutta is barred, and the Governor of Assam is the chief appellate authority.

Civil Justice.

There is no separate staff for the trial of civil cases and it is conducted by the Political Officer, his Assistants and the chief village authorities. The Political Officer is empowered to try suits up to any amount. The Assistant Political Officer shall hear and decide original civil suits up to the value of Rs. 1,000 and shall hear and decide appeals from the decision of the chief village authority up to a value of Rs. 500.

The Governor or Political Officer may, on application or otherwise, call for the proceedings of any case decided by any officer subordinate to them and pass such order as they may deem fit.

Land revenue.

There is one mauza — the Sadiya mauza—which contains 10 surveyed villages situated on the south bank of the Lohit-Brahmaputra adjoining Saikhoaghat rail head and running with the Saikhoa mauza of Lakhimpur. In these 10 villages land revenue is paid on the unit rate system, as in the cadastrally surveyed areas of Lakhimpur. Tea land at present pays an all round rate of twelve annas per bigha, while homestead land varies from Re. 1-8-0 to Re. 0-12-0, rice land from Re. 1-6-0, to Re. 0-7-0, and other lands from Re. 0-13-0 to Re 0-8-0.

In the other villages, which are unsurveyed, *basti* (homestead land) is assessed at Re. 1-2-0, *rupit* (rice land) at twelves annas and *faringati* (other land) at nine annas per bigha.

Outside the Sadiya mauza, the tribesmen Miris, Abors, Mishmis, Khamtis, Singphoes, and Nagas pay poll-tax of three rupees for each able bodied male.

Medical.

The health of the district is in charge of the Civil Surgeon, whose headquarters are at Sadiya. He is assisted by two subdivisional medical officers (Assistant Surgeons) one at Sadiya, who holds charge of the station during the Civil Surgeon's absence from headquarters on tour, and one at Pasighat who is stationed at that place, but tours in his own subdivision. There are twelve dispensaries in all, eight of them open all the year, three for about six months in the year and one *hât* dispensary open for two days in the week. As the district's sparsely populated, the number of dispensaries may at first appear lavish, but of the total number four only are regular civil dispensaries, the wants of the 2nd Battalion Assam Rifles being catered for by six, the Public Works Department on the Lohit Valley road by one. A Sub-Assistant Surgeon holds charge of each of these dispensaries and, at the isolated ones, itinerates in his neighbourhood. The Sub-Assistant Surgeon in charge of the *hât* dispensary also itinerates in the neighbourhood of Sadiya. Most of the dispensaries are equipped for the treatment of in-patients The Civil Surgeon inspects them all periodically and in the course of his tour affords medical aid to all who need it, enquiring into the health of the hamlets, and advising the inhabitants as to measures of prevention and cure of disease ; he arranges for the relief of villages in which sickness of an epidemic nature appears, and inspects all vaccination done by the vaccination staff. Maternity cases, are attended at the Sadiya Civil dispensary, to which is attached a midwife paid from the Local Fund. Her range extends to villages lying within a four-mile radius of the station.

The district is mainly backwoods, most of the locations, for stations they cannot all be called, being mere clearings in the dense forest and jungle with which the land is clad. The rainfall being heavy, the undergrowth is luxuriant and breeds all the pests that make life hard to bear. Mosquitoes, both anopheles and culex abound, as do sand-flies, damdim flies and leeches, which are all causes of disease. Malaria is fairly rife and also sores of extremities simulating the Naga sore. Fortunately a considerable number of the population live in houses with 'chang' floors or the tally of sick would be greater. The hill tribes, Abors and Mishmis, living as they do in inaccessible places and for the most part unprovided with medical aid, have to thank those self-same "chang" houses for their comparative freedom from epidemic diseases. No latrines are ever constructed by the people.

The water-supply for the most part is good, as the district is provided with clear swift-running streams. There are regions, however, where the streams are sluggish and here most sickness appears, but fortunately as the rains are frequent and heavy these streams get purified periodically and there is an abatement of disease. The people are ignorant and no concise accounts of symptoms in epidemics is ordinarily available, but influenza has lingered in the district since the universal epidemic of 1919, and sporadic cases are reported. Vaccination is confined to the civilised portions of the district. Cholera occasionally occurs on the southern banks of the Lohit, amongst tea-garden coolies and *basti* dwellers, but fortunately there has been no large epidemic. Goitre is very common among the plains people and is found among hillmen except the Naga clans.

Notwithstanding all these ills, the health of the district is fairly good, and the mortality as reported not high. A high proportion of the deaths is amongst the pauper immigrants, who seem to think Sadiya an Eldorado and persist in coming to a township that is too needy in itself to support a floating colony of beggars.

Vital statistics.

Vital statistics are reported from the one mauza, the one tea garden of the district, and from the Saw Mills areas at Murkong Selek and Laimekuri. The bulk of the district, however, does not report these occurences, so no ratio per mille can be given to convey the rise and fall of the population. But if occupancy returns can supply a criterion, the population is on the increase, for considerable bodies of able-bodied Nepali settlers frequently arrive and undoubtedly add to the number of births. The bulk of the people live in huts of bamboo and thatch, and speedy deterioration necessitates the construction of new houses on new sites. Since the material of the old houses is too decayed to use again, this occasional change of residence combined with the advantages of *chang* houses conduces to a fair amount of comfort, and by reducing the ills arising from filth, gives the district a fairly clean bill of health.

As already mentioned, there have been no regular epidemics. Figures are reliable for the epidemic diseases of cholera and influenza, but only relate to the administered portions of the district in which regular dispensaries are maintained. In all cases reported in time, Colonel Sir Leonard Roger's routine treatment has been adopted for cholera, while for influenza P. I. P. vaccine curative as well as preventive has been injected. The plains Abors, Mishmis, Khamtis and Singphoes suffered heavily in the great influenza epidemic of 1918. The two diseases cannot be said to be endemic in any particular locality and have undoubtedly been communicated by infected persons arriving in the district. Epidemics.

Other prevailing diseases in order of frequency are goitre, worms, malarial fevers and skin diseases.

Kala azar has not been met with in the district but a curious black pigmentation of the skin, mostly of the face, has been observed in a few persons who though now perfectly well, say they suffered from fever when the pigmentation began. The appearance of the skin is as though damaged by gunpowder. Venereal diseases are fortunately rare, the few cases that occur being usually of persons infected outside the district. Malaria is on the increase, which is partly explained by the influx into the district of emigrants, already infected. Many of them arrive with enlarged spleens; the anopheles mosquito does the rest.

No bezbaruas are found among the Assamese population, so there is no specific line of indigenous medical treatment. Older folk, especially amongst the Ahom population, have certain remedies mostly of a herbal nature, but no coaxing can persuade them to give any particulars of the herbs used. There are however very Indigenous treatment.

few persons that pretend to any knowledge of the cure of disease.

Most of the villagers believe in charms, and present votive offerings at the local shrines, the most celebrated being that of Balia Baba at Sadiya. Very little is known of their line of indigenous treatment followed by the Mongolian tribes. The Khamtis are however reported to have 'vaids' who have some system of medicine of their own. It is quite possible too that the Mishmis who barter herbs and various portions of the wild animals at Sadiya, may have adopted the same as remedies for sickness amongst themselves, namely, musk and the stomach of porcupine and bears. Bear's stomach is bought by Chinese from Calcutta as a cure for dyspepsia and the root "Mishmi Teeta" is used as an infusion for malarial fever and a collyrium for sore eyes. There are indigenous midwives practising their calling in the township of Sadiya but the bulk of the district's women folk receive no expert assistance. The hill tribes have their "Medicine Men," whose methods are a combination of medicine and sorcery, the latter being usually the method that appeals to the afflicted person.

Forests. The district being at present but sparsely populated the greater part is under so-called forest. No estimate of the area can be given as the district has not yet been topographically surveyed. All waste land is technically termed unclassed state forest: the stand varies from grass, reeds, and a swamp to a heavy timber, but the greater portion carries timber of some sort. The tree-bearing portion is typical mixed evergreen forest with dense undergrowth and creeper covered trees. Over the greater portion the trees are very scattered; standing singly or in groups, the intervening spaces being filled with masses of creeper or bamboos. Well stocked areas are generally of relatively small extent, but on these very large trees are found. The predominating species in the plains is "Terminalia Myriocarpa" locally called 'hollock', but on the south bank of the Brahmaputra or Lohit and along the Noa-Dehing river, Hollong, or "Dipterocarpus Pilosus," becomes the prevailing species over many areas. The foothills, as a rule, are covered with heavier timber than the plains but of the same mixed evergreen type except that Terminalia Myriocarpa does not predominate or does so very rarely.

One timber reserve and seven fuel reserves aggregating some 68 sq. miles were constituted in 1924 under the Assam Forest Regulation. In addition to these, eight areas aggregating some 354 sq. miles are notified as Protected Forests by executive order of the Political Officer. The names and areas of all the above will be found in the Appendix (page 58).

The general control of all Government forests is vested in a Deputy or Assistant Conservator whose position is defined as that of advisor on forest matters to the Political Officer. The general rules in force for control and exploitation in the other plains districts of Assam are followed except in areas which the Political Officer considers unsuitable. All persons holding land temporarily settled for cultivation are allowed to remove all forest produce needed for their own use free of any royalty. Management.

The largest Forest industry is the manufacture of tea boxes, and this is in the hands of the Assam Saw Mills and Timber Company, Limited, who have two Mills in the District. The more important of the two is the Veneer factory at Murkong Selek where three-ply boxes are manufactured from hardwood timber. For this work the species used at present exclusively is Hollock (Terminalia myriocarpa). The other mill is situated at Laimekuri, and manufactures "shooks" from soft wood timber, the species most in demand being Simul (Bombax Malabaricum). Formerly this species alone was used, but of late years supplies have become less accessible and several other species are utilised, the principal of which are Pichola (Meliosma Simplicifolia), and Borpat (Ailanthus grandis). Each of these factories consumes daily about 1,000 c. ft. of timber for working.

A lease for a period of 30 years granting the sole right to exploit timber from the plains portion of the district (excluding Fuel Reserves) was granted in 1922 to the Assam Saw Mills and Timber Company. The greater part of the timber exploited by them is used for the manufacture of tea boxes in the Mills referred to above, but quantities of hardwoods are also exploited as scantlings.

Apart from timber a substantial amount of the forest revenue of the district is obtained from cane (calamus tennis), thatching grass, and from captured elephants. The thatching grass grows on chapris in the Brahmaputra and finds a ready sale in Dibrugarh. Both this and cane are disposed of as Mahals, the purchaser paying a considerable sum for the sole right to the produce.

No regular working plan has up to the present been prepared for any forest in the district, but there is a working scheme since 1921 whereby an area sufficient to yield an amount of hardwood timber equal to the amount exploited annually is regenerated artificially each year. The annual coupe thus regenerated is a block of approximately 80 acres.

Timber trees.

The most frequent and commercially, the most valuable tree is Hollock (Terminalia Myriocarpa); the next place must at present be given to *Simul* (Bombax Malabaricum), followed by Hollong (Dipterocarpus Pilosus) and Uriam (Bischofia Javanica). Other trees valuable because of the durable or other special qualities of their timber, though occurring sporadically, are Bola (Morus Lævigata), Gunseroi (Cinnamonum Glanduliferum and Cecicodaphne), Poma (Cedrela febrifuga), Boga Poma or Silling (Chikrasia tabularis), Mekahi (Phœbe Hainesiana), Gomari (Gmelina arborea), Sam (Artocarpus Chaplasa), Jutuli (Altingia Excelsa), Phulsopa (Mangolia Spp.) and Titasopa (Mechelia Spp.). The Chalmugra tree (Taraktogenos Kurzii) also occurs in limited numbers. The most valuable tree so far found in the higher hills is the Walnut (Juglans Regia).

There are 14 Government schools in the district, namely, one Middle English school and 13 Primary schools. The Middle English school which is located at Sadiya has shown a steady increase in the number of pupils in the roll. It has a staff of 5 teachers, and it is the only school in the district in which English is taught. Of the 13 Primary schools six are in Assamese, five in Miri, and two in Abor villages. Assamese is taught in all these schools. The schools in the Assamese villages have Assamese *pandits* while those in the Miri and Abor villages with one exception have Miri *pandits*. The Assamese village schools are all flourishing, but not so those of the Miri and Abor village schools, partly owing to the want of good Miri teachers, and partly to the apathy of boys and guardians alike. The people appear to be keen on having a school and evince much interest when one is started, but this interest is apt to die when the novelty wears off. Education.

Sadiya is the headquarters of the 2nd (Lakhimpur) Battalion of the Assam Rifles, for whom permanent barracks were constructed in 1920-21. The classes recruited are Gurkhas, Cacharis, Mech, Rava and Ahoms. The battalion furnishes the cordon of outposts on the Frontier. It is officered by one Commandant and three Assistant Commandants, who are British officers of the Indian Army on deputation, by eight Subadars and nine Jemadars. The Battalion has a distinguished record in Frontier operations and supplied a very high percentage of Volunteers in the great war. Military.

APPENDIX.

List of Tables.

STATEMENT A.

LIST OF TEA GARDENS.

Serial number.	Name of garden.	Name of owner.	Mauza in which situated.	Approximate distance by road from subdivisional headquarters.	Area in acres on 31st December 1921.	Area in acres under plant (both mature and immature) on 31st December 1921.	Labour force on 31st December 1921.	Remarks.
1	2	3	4	5	6	7	8	9
				Miles.				
1	Dholla ...	The Assam Frontier Tea Company, Limited.	Sadiya ...	8	1,104·07	...	574	...

STATEMENT B.

LIST OF POST OFFICES.

Name of post office.	Mauza in which situated.
1	2
Sadiya*	**Sadiya.**
Saikwaghat*	**Sadiya.**
Kobo*	......
Pasighat*	......
Murkong Selek	......
Laimekuri	......

* Combined post and telegraph office.

STATEMENT C.

LIST OF VILLAGES IN WHICH THERE ARE THREE OR MORE PERMANENT SHOPS: —Choukham.

STATEMENT D.

LIST OF MARKETS.

Place where market is held.	Days of week on which held.
1	2
Sadiya	Held daily.
Saikwa	Friday and Saturday.
Pasighat	Sunday and Thursday.

TABLE I.

Average Maximum and Minimum Temperatures registered at Sadiya.

	January.	February.	March.	April.	May.	June.	July.	August.	September.	October.	November.	December.	Annual mean.
1	2	3	4	5	6	7	8	9	10	11	12	13	14
Maximum Temperature 1921 ...	66·46	74·71	82·64	86·23	86·08	88·5	89·19	84	89·3	88·29	78·76	72·96	81·67
1922 ...	71·71	76·83	76·78	87·23	85·93	87.73	88·90	87·26	89·58	89·63	79·50	71·97	...
1923 ...	64·81	69·90	80·00	79·63	78·00	85·80	86·60	88·61	89·91	85·68	81·57	73·12	...
1924 ...	68·61	71·51	78·33	77·30	80·71	86·96	86·26	84·83	86·13	85·00	77·23	75·43	...
Minimum Temperature 1921 ...	50·77	52·57	64·23	67·86	74 00	77·10	76·12	75·26	73·9	70·61	58·2	50·71	65·95
1922 ...	49·67	46·83	55·86	63·93	71·46	74·50	76·23	76·88	76·10	68·87	57·80	49·07	...
1923 ...	49·74	54·50	59·93	65·73	70·74	75·80	77·17	79·13	74·73	68·49	59·76	51·03	...
1924 ...	50·74	34·79	61·84	66·80	69·46	76·96	76·87	76·51	74·96	71·81	61·13	52·36	...

The figures represent the averages for 1921 only. Previously no records were kept.

TABLE II.

Rainfall.

The number of years for which the average has been calculated is shown against the name of each station.

Months.	Average rainfall in inches.	
	Sadiya (18 years).	Pasighat (6 years).
1	2	3
January	2·60	1·36
February	4·14	3·70
March	6·24	7·54
April	11·45	11·22
May	12·71	17·10
June	21·72	43·34
July	21·09	43·25
August	18·67	24·71
September	12·89	18·02
October	5·65	13·93
November	0·71	0·92
December	1·21	0·84
Annual ...	119·08	186·58

TABLE III.

Distribution of population.

Mauza.		Population in 1921.	Population in 1911.	Difference.	Area in square miles.	Population per square mile in 1921.	Number of persons censused in tea gardens in 1921.
1		2	3	4	5	6	7
Sadiya Subdivision	...	25,949	...	...	(a)	...	...
Sadiya Town ...	...	3,590	...	...	(a)	...	...
Sadiya Mauza ...	...	4,271	...	...	130·15	33	1,068
Unsettled area ...	...	18,088	...	...	(a)	...	...
Pasighat Subdivision	...	13,582	..	...	(a)	...	...
Total	...	39,531	16,996	+22,535	389·00	9	1,068

(a) Areas not available.

TABLE IV.

General statistics of population.

Particulars.		Sadiya Subdivision.		Pasighat Subdivision.		Total district.		
		Males.	Females.	Males.	Females.	Persons.	Males.	Females.
1		2	3	4	5	6	7	8
Population—								
1921 ...	...	14,687	11,262	7,320	6,262	39,531	22,007	17,524
1911 ...	...	...	...	...	...	16,996	...	...
Variation—								
1911—1921 ...	...	...	...	..	...	+22,535	...	...

TABLES IV—*contd*.

Particulars.	Sadiya Sub-division		Pasighat Subdivision.		Total districts.		
	Males.	Females	Males	Females.	Persons	Males.	Females.
1	2	3	4	5	6	7	8
Religion—							
Total Hindus .	..				19,255	11,449	7,806
Animists					16,548	8,411	8,137
Muhammadans					573	427	146
Total Christians	.		...		300	173	127
(I) Anglican Com munion.					31	22	9
(II) Baptist					235	127	108
(III) Presbyterian			.		4	4	..
(IV) Roman Catholic ..				.	3	3	...
Other Religions ...			...	.	2,955	1,647	1,308
Civil condition—							
Unmarried -	.				20,599	11,932	8,667
Married					15,552	8,591	6,961
Widowed			...		3,380	1,484	1,896
Literacy—							
Literate ...	.	.	...		2,482	2,343	139
Literate in English	...		...		428	413	15
Illiterate ...				...	37,049	19,684	17,365
Languages spoken—							
Abor .		..			11,526	5,730	5,796
Assamese					6,364	3,827	2,537

TABLE IV—*concld.*

Particulars.	Sadiya Sub-division.		Pasighat Subdivision.		Total districts.		
	Males.	Females.	Males.	Females.	Persons.	Males.	Females.
1	2	3	4	5	6	7	
Languages spoken—contd.—							
Bengali ..		...	...		1,040	664	376
Kachin or Singpho				...	1,424	730	694
Khamti					2,085	1,075	1,010
Manipur, Meithei Kathe or Ponna		...			104	94	10
Miri .			...		4,719	2,339	2,380
Mishmi	...			...	778	417	361
Naga (unspecified)			...	...	208	143	65
Gond .		...	...		208	120	88
Gurung .	...			...	129	72	57
Hindi	...	...	...	...	2,830	1,752	1,078
Khambu	...			...	309	193	116
Kurukh or Oraon ..	...	...			339	180	159
Limbu				...	242	134	108
Magari ...			...	...	556	366	190
Mundari ..	...	...	...	...	441	249	192
Nepali . ..			...	...	3,568	2,224	1,344
Newari ..		...		...	108	86	22
Oriya ...	...	...	...	...	1,135	639	496
Bhotia of Tibet ...	...	...		...	579	261	318

TABLE V.

Birth place, race, caste and occupation.

Particulars.	Persons.	Males.	Females.
1	2	3	4
Birthplace.			
Born in the district ...	26,017	13,393	12,624
Ditto other parts of province	123	71	52
Ditto Bengal	739	516	223
Ditto Bihar and Orissa ...	3,623	2,221	1,402
Ditto Central Provinces and Berar.	829	498	331
Ditto Madras	598	303	295
Ditto United Provinces ...	310	184	156
Ditto Nepal	4,243	2,822	1,421
Ditto elsewhere ...	3,019	1,999	1,020
Race and caste.			
Abor	11,489	5,695	5,794
Ahom	4,775	2,607	2,168
Brahman	783	519	264
Chamar	135	78	57
Chutiya	267	148	119
Goala	329	203	126
Kachari	407	232	175
Kaibartha	436	200	236
Khamti	1,460	785	675
Kurmi	108	108	...

TABLE V—*concld.*

Particulars.	Persons.	Males.	Females.
1	2	3	4
Race and caste—concld.			
Lohar	92	70	22
Miri	4,588	2,423	2,165
Mishmi	771	414	357
Munda	391	219	172
Nadiyal	231	118	113
Naga	220	148	72
Oraon	341	185	156
Orya (unspecified)	95	64	31
Rajput (Chhattri)	997	652	345
Santal	283	254	29
Singpho	1,463	768	695
Sonwal	426	213	213
Tanti	1,002	268	234
Teli or Tili	108	73	35
Sheikh	445	324	121
Occupation.			
Workers	16,925	14,287	2,638
Dependents	22,606	7,720	14,886
Total supported.			
Landlord	1	1	...
Ordinary cultivators	10,929	9,501	1,428
Field labourers	143	113	30
On tea gardens	940	495	445
In fisheries	3	3	...

TABLE VI.

Crop Statistics.

Particulars.	1916-17.	1917-18.	1918-19.	1919-20.	1920-21.	1921-22.	1922-23.	1923-24.	1924-25.	1925-26.	1926-27.	1927-28.	1928-29.	1929-30.	1930-31.	1931-32.
1	2	3	4	5	6	7	8	9	10	11	12	13	14	15	16	17
	Acres.	Acres.	Acres.	Acres.	Acres.	Acres.	Acres.	Acres.								
Total cropped area	7,632	8,367	9,873	8,132	6,164	8,299	8 661	9,351								
Rice	4,903	5,822	6,771	6,072	6,081	6,086	6,518	6,511								
Mustard	370	627	661	688	693	660	665	1,082								
Sugarcane	638	733	670	634	639	668	701	674								
Pulse	539	152	151	96	126	133	139	174								
All other crops	1,193	1,053	1,090	732	796	763	638	911								

TABLE VI—*concld.*

Crop Statistics—concld.

Particulars.	1920.	1921.	1922.	1923.	1924.	1925.	1926.	1927.	1928.	1929.	1930.	1931.	1932.
1	2	3	4	5	6	7	8	9	10	11	12	13	14
TEA.	Acres.	Acres.	Acres.	Acres.	Acres.								
Number of gardens	1	1											
Area in acres	670	670	1,292·10	1,292·10	1,293·10								
Area under plant. held by European ..	412	412	423	434	434								
Area under plant. held by Indian ...	...	...	...	.	. .								
Outturn in lbs.	173,634	150,616	160,786	193,328	259,108								
Labour force	624	624	656	670	656								
Labourers including dependents imported during the year.	634	574	545	519	595								

TABLE VII.

Regular Reserved Forests—Local Government Notification No. 765R.—772R., dated the 31st March 1923.

			Sq. mile.
1. Sadiya Station and Military Fuel Reserve East Block	...	...	13·75
2. Sadiya Station and Military Fuel Reserve West Block	...	...	3·43
3. Kumsong Fuel Reserve	...	...	4·37
4. Sengajan Fuel Reserve	...	...	6·25
5. Hologaon Fuel Reserve	...	...	1·09
6. Kukuramara Fuel Reserve	...	...	1·64
7. Hakati Fuel Reserve	...	...	2·59
8. Poba Timber Reserve	...	...	35·23
	Total	...	68·35

Reserved Forests protected by the Executive Orders of the Political Officer, Sadiya.

				Sq. mile.
1. Kerim Timber Reserve		...	...	14·91
2. Deopani	,,	...	...	54·93
3. Paya	,,	...	...	92·00
4. Manubum	,,	...	...	73·60
5. Namsai	,,	...	...	10·78
5. Namphuk	,,	...	...	22·00
7. Pasighat	,,	...	...	26·20
8. Gali	,,	...	...	60·00
		Total	...	354·42

TABLE

Outturn of Timber and Fuel

Details.		1921-22.	1922-23.	1923-24.
1		2	3	4
RESERVED AND PROTECTED FORESTS.				
Area in square miles		245·59	422·77	422·77
Outturn—(Government and purchasers only)—				
Timber	C. ft.	Nil	260,217	499,346
Fuel	C. ft.	Nil	3,780	16,078
Thatch	Rs.	Nil	Nil	6
Cane	Rs.	Nil	Nil	19
UNCLASSED STATE FORESTS.				
Area in square miles		Unknown.		
Outturn—(Government and purchasers only)—				
Timber	C.ft.	624,842	551,140	550,948
Fuel	C.ft.	142,102	74,566	78,730
Cane	Rs.	32,500	12,538	20,833
Elephants	Rs.	Nil	85,500	20,300(a)
Thatch	Rs.	4,539	14,288	11,235
Bamboos	Rs.	123	98	193
Beeswax	Rs.	363	351	197
Ekra	Rs.	1	18	24
Elephant Tusk	Rs.	Nil	Nil	319
Forest receipt	Rs.	55,699	1,08,742	86,229
„ expenditure	Rs.	62,737	58,967	41,979
Surplus	Rs.	−7,038(b)	49,775	44,250

Note—(a) Includes Rs. 8,300 sale proceeds of
(b) In 1921-22 there was a

VIII.

and value of Minor Forest Produce.

1924-25.	1925-26.	1926-27.	1927-28.	1928-29.	1929-30.	1930-31. (July to March).	1931-32.
5	6	7	8	9	10	11	12

three Departmental elephants.
deficit of Rs. 7,093.

TABLE IX.

Prices of food staples in seers obtainable per rupee.

—		Sadiya.			Pasighat.		
		Common rice.	Salt.	Matikalai.	Common rice.	Salt.	Matikalai.
1		2	3*	4	5	6	7
		Seers.	Seers.	Seers.	Seers.		
1915	2nd week of February ...	...	...	...	...	Not available.	Not available.
	Ditto August ...	6½	10	8	5		
1916	Ditto February ...	6½	7½	8	5		
	Ditto August ..	7	8	8	4½		
1917	Ditto February ...	6½	8	8½	5		
	Ditto August ...	6½	7	8	5½		
1918	Ditto February ...	7½	6½	10	6		
	Ditto August ..	6½	7	9	5½		
1919	Ditto February ...	6½	8	5½	4¾		
	Ditto August ...	5	6	4¾	5		
1920	Ditto February ...	4½	8	5	5		
	Ditto August ...	4	5	5½	4		
1921	Ditto February ...	4¾	8	6½	4		
	Ditto August ...	4¾	5½	7	4		
1922	Ditto February ...	5½	8	8	5		
	Ditto August ...	5	8	7	5		
1923	Ditto February ...	5½	8	6·8	5		
	Ditto August ...	6	7	6·4	5½		
1924	Ditto February ...	6	7	7	5½		
	Ditto August ...	5	8	7	5½		
1925	Ditto February ...	5½	8	7	5		
	Ditto August ...						
1926	Ditto February ...						
	Ditto August ...						

TABLE IX—*concld.*

—	Sadiya.			Pasighat.		
	Common rice.	Salt.	Matika-lai.	Common rice.	Salt.	Matika-lai.
1	2	3	4	5	6	7
	Seers.	Seers.	Seers.	Seers.		
1927 2nd week of February ..						
1927 Ditto August ...						
1928 Ditto February ...						
1928 Ditto August ...						
1929 Ditto February ...						
1929 Ditto August ...						
1930 Ditto February ...						
1930 Ditto August ...						
1931 Ditto February ...						
1931 Ditto August ...						
1932 Ditto February ...						
1932 Ditto August ...						

TABLE

Statistics of Criminal

Heads of crime.	1915.		1916.		1917.	
	True.	Detected.	True.	Detected.	True.	Detected.
1	2	3	4	5	6	7
CRIMINAL JUSTICE.						
Number of cases.						
(i) Rioting or unlawful assembly, sections 143-153, 157, 158 and 159.	1	1	...	...	...	...
(ii) Other offences against the State, public tranquillity, etc.	...	...	...	...	1	1
(iii) Murder, attempt at murder and culpable homicide, sections 302-304, 307, 308 and 396.	...	...	1	...	3	3
(iv) Grievous hurt and hurt by dangerous weapon, sections 324-326, 329, 331, 333 and 335.	7	7	9	9	11	11
(v) Serious criminal force, sections 353, 354, 356 and 357.	13	13	13	13	28	28
(vi) Other serious offences against the person	4	4	...	...	...	...
(vii) Dacoity, sections 395, 397 and 398 ...	...	...	...	...	...	...
(viii) Serious mischief, including mischief by killing, poisoning or maiming any animal, sections 270, 281, 282, 428, 429, 430-433 and 435-440.	3	3	23	23	50	50
(ix) House breaking and serious house trespass, sections 449-452, 454, 455 and 457-460.	8	8	3	3	14	14
(x) Wrongful restraint and confinement, sections 341-344.	...	...	...	...	...	...
(xi) Other serious offences against the person and property or against property.	11	11	15	15	16	16
(xii) Theft, sections 379—382	31	23	23	19	24	20
(xiii) Receiving stolen property, sections 411 and 414.	1	1	8	8	1	1
(xiv) Lurking and criminal house-trespass, sections 453, 456, 447 and 448.	...	...	7	7	14	14
(xv) Other minor offences against property ...	23	23	12	12	7	7
Total	103	94	114	109	169	165

X.

and Civil Justice.

1918.		1919.		1920.		1921.		1922.		1923.	
True.	Detected.	True.	Detected.	True.	Detected.	True.	Detected.	True.	Detected.	True.	Detected.
8	9	10	11	12	13	14	15	16	17	18	19
...	..	...	...	4	4	1	1	...	...	1	1
...	...	1	1	...	...	...	...	4	4	1	
...	...	3	3	2	2	3	3	4	4	1	1
12	12	4	4	4	4	6	6	7	7	14	14
30	39	43	43	40	40	41	41	44	44	54	54
1	1	2	2	3	3	13	13	10	10	2	2
...	...	...	...	...	...	1	1	1	1	...	...
44	44	65	65	9	9	4	4	5	5	20	20
10	10	9	9	11	11	1	1	2	2	8	8
...	...	1	1	...	..	...	...	.	...	1	1
12	13	4	4	9	9	..	...	...	...	...	...
28	24	37	32	31	24	20	29	35	35	32	32
...	...	6	6	1	1	3	3	11	11		6
12	10	4	4	2	2	3	3	5	5		5
6	6	9	9	2	2	9	9	11	11	19	19
164	158	188	183	118	111	114	114	139	139	164	164

TABLE X.

Statistics of Criminal and Civil Justice—concld.

Heads of crime.	1915.	1916.	1917	1918.	1919.	1920.	1921.	1922.	1923.	1924.	1925.	1926.	1927.	1928.	1929.	1930.	1931.	1932.
1	2	3	4	5	6	7	8	9	10	11	12	13	14	15	16	17	18	19
CIVIL JUSTICE.																		
Number of suits for money and moveable	264	251	306	221	246	193	352	258	216	162	...	..	...	...	...	...	..	...

TABLE XI.

Fluctuations in settled area.

Particulars.	1913-14.	1914-15.	1915-16.	1916-17.	1917-18.	1918-19.	1919-20.	1920-21.	1921-22.	1922-23.	1923-24.	1924-25.	1925-26.	1926-27.	1927-28.	1928-29.	1929-30.	1930-31.	1931-32.
1	2	3	4	5	6	7	8	9	10	11	12	13	14	15	16	17	18	19	20
Settled area (acres)	2,331	3,004	8,496	8,865	9,821	8,732	8,837	9,346	9,855	10,938	11,459	...	*...	...	...	...	...	...	...
Area excluded from settlement (acres).	428	4,715	1,739	972	1,040	1,798	1,834	1,168	1,190	896	979	...	...	...	...	...	...	...	...
Area included in settlement (acres).	890	5,782	2,108	2,011	1,356	1,222	1,790	2,067	1,667	1,969	1,510	...	...	...	...	...	...	...	...
Revenue demand .	Rs. 5,478	Rs. 6,878	Rs. 18,795	Rs. 19,344	Rs. 21,329	Rs. 19,183	Rs. 19,609	Rs. 20,346	Rs. 21,516	Rs. 23,518	Rs. 24,538	...	...	...	...	...	...	...	...

The Sadiya mauza until 1914-15 included only the north bank of the Brahmaputra and Lohit Brahmaputra in the Sadiya Frontier Tract. In 1915-16 the portion of the Saikwa mauza (Lakhimpur) falling within the boundary of the Sadiya Frontier Tract District created in 1913 was transferred to the Sadiya mauza of the Sadiya Frontier Tract.

TABLE

Miscellaneous

Particulars.	1914-15.	1915-16.	1916-17.	1917-18.	1918-19.	1919-20.
1	2	3	4	5	6	7
	Rs.	Rs.	Rs.	Rs.	Rs.	Rs.
Poll-tax	[illegible],624	7,562	9,901	10,603	10,263	10,432
Fisheries	192	200	300	200	368	400
Total	6,816	7,762	10,201	10,803	10,631	10,832

TABLE

Finance

Principal heads.	1912-13.	1913-14.	1914-15.	1915-16.	1916-17.	1917-18.
1	2	3	4	5	6	7
	Rs.	Rs.	Rs.	Rs.	Rs.	Rs.
Land Revenue (ordinary) ...	...	...	6,834	18,786	10,844	19,055
Land Revenue (Miscellaneous)...	4,803	6,897	6,616	7,762	10,201	10,803
Provincial rates	...	...	430	1,184	1,229	1,356
Judicial stamps	...	...	...	7,223	8,831	...
Non-judicial stamps ..	...	...	...	...	...	226
Opium	...	...	...	30,264	23,580	15,120
Country spirit	...	...	...	6,804	5,825	9,180
Ganja	...	...	...	1,64	1,080	1,452
Other heads of excise ...	...	...	...	100	100	150
Assessed taxes	...	...	580	2,806	3,426	5,797
Registration	...	...	...	...	...	...
Forests	...	...	...	80,065	81,875	45,601
Total ...	.	...	..	...	...	...

XII.

Land Revenue.

1920-21.	1921-22.	1922-23.	1923-24.	1924-25.	1925-26.	1926-27.	1927-28.	1928-29.	1929-30.	1930-31.	1931-32.
8	9	10	11	12	13	14	15	16	17	18	19
Rs.	Rs.	Rs.	Rs.								
11,728	15,140	16,364	16,730								
100	350	400	480								
11,828	15,490	16,764	17,210								

XIII.

Receipts.

1918-19.	1919-20.	1920-21.	1921-22.	1922-23.	1923-24.	1924-25.	1925-26.	1926-27.	1927-28.	1928-29.	1929-30.	1930-31.	1931-32.
8	9	10	11	12	13	14	15	16	17	18	19	20	21
Rs.	Rs.	Rs.	Rs.	Rs.	Rs.								
20,341	19,809	20,410	21,516	23,518	24,533								
10,651	10,832	11,828	3,166	4,188	4,457								
1,284	1,231	1,290	1,366	1,473	1,536								
3,331	5,093	5,609	...	...	...								
315	518	428	...	...	...								
19,980	21,730	62,356	80,110	81,519	83,700								
9,240	9,300	33,161	18,580	21,611	19,660								
1,920	600	2,640	2,920	3,500	2,750								
100	100	160	160	160	160								
5,916	4,253	4,968	10,944	11,388	11,597								
36	16	16	...	...	...								
67,098	61,437	51,072	...	...	...								
...	...	...	...	...	...	...	...	...	...	...	...	...	...

TABLE

Land

Particulars.	1915-16.	1916-17.	1917-18.	1918-19.	1919-20.
1	2	3	4	5	6
		Acres.	Acres.	Acres.	Acres.
Total land settled for cultivation of ordinary crops.	Not available.	7,632	8,357	9,278	8,132
Held on ordinary tenures		7,632	8,357	9,278	8,132
Held revenue free (*Lakhiraj*)		Nil	Nil	Nil	Nil
Held at half rates (*Nisf-khiraj*) ...		Nil	Nil	Nil	Nil
Total land settled for cultivation of special staples.		4,903	5,823	6.771	6,073
Area of free simple and commuted grants		Nil	Nil	Nil	
Area settled on 30 years' lease ...		Nil	Nil	Nil	Nil
Area held under ordinary rules or resettled on expiry of 30 years' lease.		Nil	Nil	Nil	Nil
Total land settled under other tenures ...		Nil	Nil	Nil	Nil
Total settled area of the district ...		7,632	8,357	9,273	8,136
Total unsettled area of the district ...		763	708	690	580

XIV.

Tenures.

1920-21.	1921-22.	1922-23.	1923-24.	1924-25.	1925-26.	1926-27.	1927-28.	1928-29.	1929-30.	1930-31.	1931-32.
7	8	9	10	11	12	13	14	15	16	17	18
Acres.	Acres.	Acres.	Acres.								
6,840	8,133	8,661	9,351								
8,840	8,133	8,661	9,351								
Nil	Nil	Nil	Nil								
Nil	Nil	Nil	Nil								
Nil	Nil	Nil	Nil								
Nil	Nil	Nil	Nil								
6,840	8,133	8,661	9,351								

TABLE

Excise

Principal heads.	1914-15.	1915-16.	1916-17.	1917-18.	1918-19.	1919-20.	1920-21.
1	2	3	4	5	6	7	8
SADIYA FRONTIER TRACT.							
Number of Opium shops ...	4	4	4	6	6	7	7
Amount paid for licenses ...	...	Rs. 40,264	Rs. 23,580	Rs. 15,120	Rs. 19,920	Rs. 21,720	Rs. 28,028
	Mds. sr.	Mds. sr.	Mds. sr.	Mds. sr.	Mds. sr.	Mds. sr.	Mds. sr.
Opium issued	...	32 26	32 0	27 16	29 39	32 9	32 11
Duty on opium sold		Not available					Rs. 54,206
Number of *ganja* shops ...	1	1	1	1	1	1	1
Amount paid for licenses ...	Rs. ...	Rs. 1,044	Rs. 1,680	Rs. 1,452	Rs. 1,920	Rs. 600	Rs. 1,420
	Mds. sr.	Mds. sr.	Mds. sr.	Mds. sr.	Mds. sr.	Mds. sr.	Mds. sr.
Ganja issued	...	1 28	1 35	1 22	1 28	1 32	1 31
Duty on *ganja* sold		Not available.					1,490
Number of country spirit retail shops.	2	2	4	3	3	3	4
Amount paid for licenses ...	...	Rs. 6,604	Rs. 5,825	Rs. 9,160	Rs. 9,340	Rs. 9,300	Rs. as. 12,576 12
Duty on liquor issued		Not available.					20,524 6
Liquor issued (L. P. gallons) ..	...	1,104	1,807	2,898	2,998	4,918	4,706
Number of Foreign liquor shops	1	1	1	1	1	1	2
Amount paid for licenses ...	...	Rs. 100	Rs. 100	Rs. 150	Rs. 100	Rs. 100	Rs. 160

XV.

statistics.

1921-22.	1922-23.	1923-24.	1924-25.	1925-26.	1926-27.	1927-28.	1928-29.	1929-30.	1930-31.	1931-32.
9	10	11	12	13	14	15	16	17	18	19
7	7	7								
Rs. 31,825	Rs. 39,354	Rs. 47,125								
Mds. sr.	Mds. sr.	Mds. sr.								
21 33	23 12	21 17								
Rs. 57,285	Rs. 42,165	Rs. 38,565								
1	1	1								
Rs. 1,460	Rs. 2,100	Rs. 1,650								
Mds. sr.	Mds. sr.	Mds. sr.								
1 33	1 30	1 15								
Rs. 1,460	Rs. 1,400	Rs. 1,100								
3	3	3								
Rs. as. 6,085 11	Rs. as. 5,336 2	Rs. 4,455								
12,445 0	16,275 0	15,175								
2,527 0	2,189 0	1,600								
2	2	2								
Rs. 160	Rs. 160	Rs. 160								

TABLE XVI.

Income and expenditure of Sadiya Local Fund for the year **1923-24.**

Sources of income.	Income. 1923-24.			Heads of expenditure.	Expenditure. 1923-24.		
1	2			3	4		
	Rs.	a.	p.		Rs.	a.	p.
1. Opening balance ...	33,549	15	8	1. Administration ...	1,793	14	0
2. Ground rent ...	2,720	1	0	2. Conservancy ...	3,056	3	4
3. Pounds ...	2,532	6	5	3. Public Works ...	3,043	9	6
4. Fees from markets	6,274	4	0	4. Medical and Sanitation.	1,610	8	0
5. Grants from Government.	400	0	0	5. Deposits and advances.	29,119	6	2
6. Rent of houses, etc.	3,190	8	0	6. Other heads ...	3,856	15	11
7. Percentage on auction sales of *teeta*, musk, etc.	7,825	9	1	Total ...	42,479	8	11
Other sources ...	7,887	10	11	Closing balance	21,900	13	9
Total ...	64,380	6	8	Total ...	64,380	6	8

TABLE XVII.

Strength of Police Force.

Particulars.	1911.	1931.
1	2	3
CIVIL POLICE.		
SUPERVISING STAFF.		
District and Assistant Superintendents...	...	...
Inspectors	...	...
SUBORDINATE STAFF.		
Sub-Inspectors	..	1
Head constables...	...	1
Constables	...	8
Union and Municipal Police	...	...
MILITARY POLICE.		
Officers	...	16
Men	...	781
Total expenditure ...	...	3,60,900 8 6*

* Civil Police expenditure is included in the expenditure of Lakhimpur district.

TABLE XVIII.

Assam Rifles Outposts.

Name of station or outpost.	Strength.
1	2
Headquarters, Sadiya	8 platoons.*
Denning	3 sections.
Nisamghat	1 platoon.
Kobo	1 section.
Pasighat	2 platoons.
Rotung	1 platoon.
Yembung	2 sections.
Tirap	1 platoon.

* Two of these platoons are nominal only, having been reduced temporarily as a measure of economy, and two more are "Headquarters platoons" of employed men.

TABLE XIX.

Education.

Particulars	1914-15.	1915-16.	1916-17	1917-18	1918-19	1919-20	1920-21	1921-22.	1922-23.	1923-24	1924-25.	1925-26	1926-27	1927-28	1928-29	1929-30	1930-31	1931-32
1	2	3	4	5	6	7	8	9	10	11	12	13	14	15	16	17	18	19
Middle English School—																		
Number	1	1	1	1	1	1	1	1	1	1								
Number of boys ...	Figures not available	63	65	73	87	94	97	88	93	86				...			-	
Lower Primary Schools—																		
Number ...	4	12	12	12	13	14	14	14	14	14			.				...	
Number of boys reading in 3 upper classes*						..	148	160	145	148								
Number of boys reading in lower classes*			.				270	251	210	250	.	...			..			

* Figures from 1914-15 to 1919-20 are not available.

TABLE XX.

Educational Finance.

Particulars.	Number of institutions.	Expenditure on institutions maintained or aided by Public Funds in 1920-21 from: Provincial Revenue.	District and Municipal Funds.	Fees.	Other sources.	Total.	Expenditure pupil.
1	2	3	4	5	6	7	8
		Rs.		Rs.		Rs.	Rs. a. p.
Middle English School.	1	3,427	...	435	...	3,862	20 3 3
Lower Primary Schools.	13	3,538	..	...		3,538	6 7 5
Total ...	14	6,965	...	435	...	7,400	14 5 11

TABLE XXI.

Medical.

Particulars.	Sadiya subdivision.		Pasighat subdivision.		Total district.	
	1911.	1921.	1911.	1921.	1911.	1921.
1	2	3	4	5	6	7
Number of dispensaries ...	...	3	...	3	...	6
Daily average number of in-door patients.	...	12·62	...	7·44	...	20·06
Daily average number of out-door patients.	...	26·22	...	28·03	...	54·25
Cases treated	...	7,096	...	7,310	...	15,306
Operations performed ...	...	1,400	...	683	...	2,083
		Rs.		Rs.		Rs.
Total income	...	9,978	...	5,638	...	15,616
Income from Government ...	...	9,396	...	5,638	...	15,034
Income from Local and Municipal funds.	...	...	...	...	...	...
Subscriptions	...	167	...	...	...	167
Total expenditure	...	9,978	...	5,638	...	15,616
Expenditure on establishment...	...	6,911	...	4,388	...	11,299
Ratio per mille of persons successfully vaccinated.	...	46·09	...	39·75	...	43·93
		Rs. a. p.		Rs. a. p.		Rs. a. p.
Cost per case	...	0 8 1	...	1 2 11	...	0 11 4

TABLE XXII.

TABLE

Dispen

Name of Dispensaries.	1914.		1915.		1916.	
	Total cost.	Cases treated.	Total cost.	Cases treated.	Total cost.	Cases treated.
1	2	3	4	5	6	7
TRAVELLING DISPENSARIES.						
Sadiya	...	...	...	...	...	...
ORDINARY DISPENSARY.						
Sadiya	...	7,458	...	8,747	3,151	6,468
Nisamghat	...	...	...	...	—	80
Pasighat	...	3,721	...	3,412	4,849	2,805
Balek-Rotung	...	3,065	...	797	644	919
Kobo	...	1,386	...	1,840	1,028	1,343

Name of Dispensaries.	1922.		1923.		1924.		1925.		1926.	
	Total cost.	Cases treated.	Total cost.	Cases treated.	Total cost.	Cases treated.	Total cost.	Cases treated.	Total cost.	Cases treated.
	18	19	20	21	22	23	24	25	26	27
TRAVELLING DISPENSARIES.										
Sadiya	1,787	2,895	1,824	4,036	1,225	2,609	...	...	...	...
ORDINARY DISPENSARIES.										
Sadiya	8,522	5,275	9,447	4,582	9,200	4,264	...	...	...	...
Nisamghat	...	440	* 34	590	...	503	...	...	...	...
Airi river and Amily ...	...	585	...	183	...	...	...	...	—	...
Denning	...	...	...	...	1,568	2,345	...	...	...	...
Tirap	...	...	—	...	17	613	...	...	...	...
Pasighat	[illegible]	4,780	5,448	4,600	5,011	4,671	...	...	...	...
Balek-Rotung	...	626	9	1,204	5	764	...	...	...	...
Kobo	2,720	1,090	2,665	1,517	1,481	1,348	—	...	...	...

* Rupees 34 represents cost of both Nisamghat and Airi river and Amily.

XXII.

saries.

1917.		1918.		1919.		1920.		1921.	
Total cost.	Cases treated.	Total cost.	Cases treated.	Total cost.	Cases treated.	Total cost.	Cases treated.	Total cost.	Cases treated.
8	9	10	11	12	13	14	15	16	17
...	...	...	...	102	904	1,511	995	1,772	2,648
5,979	7,173	6,968	5,617	4,220	4,961	4,055	5,716	5,206	5,074
...	135	..	417	...	591	...	1,563	...	279
4,699	2,603	5,880	3,000	2,967	5,841	3,704	3,690	3,261	4,162
...	700	..	806	...	292	...	760	...	331
1,543	1,397	698	290	550	523	2,067	2,007	2,287	2,317

1927.		1928.		1929.		1930.		1931.		1932.	
Total cost.	Cases treated.	Total cost.	Cases treated.	Total cost.	Cases treated.	Total cost.	Cases treated.	Total cost.	Cases treated.	Total cost.	Cases treated.
28	29	30	31	32	33	34	35	36	37	38	39
...	...	...	...	...	...	...	...	...	...	...	...
...	...	...	...	...	...	...	...	...	...	...	..
...	...	...	...	...	...	...	...	...	...	...	...
...	...	...	...	...	...	...	...	...	...	...	...
...	...	...	...	...	...	...	...	...	...	...	...
...	...	...	...	...	...	...	...	...	...	...	...
...	...	...	...	...	...	...	...	...	...	..	...
...	...	...	...	...	...	...	...	...	...	...	...
...	...	...	...	...	...	...	...	...	...	...	...

ANNEXURE A.

Notes on the Geology of the Sadiya Frontier Tract.

Compiled by P. Evans, Esq. of the Assam Oil Company, Ltd.

1. The Sadiya Frontier Tract may be divided into four different portions marked by special distinguishing geological features :—

(*a*) The hill ranges north west and north of Sadiya, which form the eastern continuation of the Himalayas.

(*b*) The hill ranges east of Brahmakund lying across the head of the Assam Valley.

(*c*) The lower ranges of Manabum, Misobum and the Patkois lying some distance south-east of Sadiya.

(*d*) The large alluvial plain of the Brahmaputra and its tributaries, of which Sadiya is approximately the central point.

2. Although these areas are best described separately, it will be convenient first to consider the general sequence of strata in the district. The rocks composing the various ranges of hills differ greatly in geological age ; one large group (known as the Archean) is of very great geological antiquity, whilst another large group is almost the youngest of the big geological deposits. Representatives of intermediate ages are also found, but these cover a much smaller area.

STRATIGRAPHY.

3. The rocks may be classified as follows :—

V. Recent	... ...	River alluvium.
IV. (Probably) Pleistocene	...	Older alluvial deposits.
III. Tertiary (Eocene to Pliocene).		Dihing Series.
		Tipam ,,
		Coal Measure ,,
		Disang ,,
II. Gondwana (Permo-Carboniferous, etc.).		Damuda Series, etc.
I. Metamorphic (Pre-cambrian).		Various rocks of great geological age.

4. The oldest rocks are schists, gneisses, quartzites, slates and limestones. Comparatively little is known about them, but it is fairly certain that many, if not all, of these rocks are of Archean

or Pre-Cambrian age—*i.e.*, they belong to the oldest known geological system, and are equivalent to rocks found elsewhere through out a large part of India.

5. The rocks which immediately follow in the geological scale of age are not known to occur in the Frontier Tracts and the next system represented is the much newer Gondwana system. Rocks of this age occur in large areas in Bengal and elsewhere, and amongst them are included the coal seams of the large Indian coalfields. In the Sadiya Frontier Tract, however, the rocks are mostly sandstones, quartzites, and shales, with but little coal. In the Abor country a great thickness of volcanic rocks are found interspersed in this series; of these rocks the most common are basaltic lavas, but volcanic "ashes" (*i.e.*, tuffs) are also found. The rocks have been correlated with the Damuda series—which is the subdivision of the Lower Gondwanas containing the actual workable seams of the Bengal coalfields. From the evidence of boulders containing marine fossils found in the Subansiri river it appears that also the Lower Productus Limestone occurs somewhere in the hills.

6. Above the Gondwana beds there occurs another break in the geological sequence, and the next strata are of Tertiary age. The Tertiary rocks have been investigated in more detail than the older beds, and have been subdivided into a number of series and groups :—

(*a*) Of the four different series the *Disang Series*, named after a river in the hills south-west of the Sadiya Frontier Tract, is the oldest, and possibly includes some beds of Cretaceous age as well as Lower Tertiary rocks (Eocene Oligocene). The Disang series is made up of many thousands of feet of grey shale with interbedded flaggy sandstones, sandy shales and thin impure limestones.

(*b*) The Disang rocks grade into a series of sandstones, shales, mudstones, etc., which is termed the *Coal Measure Series*. This series is probably over 10,000 feet thick and in it there occur many thin beds of coal and carbonaceous shale. Except in the lower part of the series mottled and blue clays are common; in the upper part there occurs in addition to the thin coals already mentioned a group of fairly thick coal seams, which is traceable for a considerable distance in the Frontier Tracts and in the neighbouring portion of the Lakhimpur district. In this latter district the seams are extensively worked in the various collieries of the Assam Railway and Trading Company and it was the occurrence of these seams that led to the series receiving its name.

(*c*) Over the Coal Measures occurs the *Tipam Series*, so named from the Tipam hills near Jaipur (Lakhimpur). This series is also rather over 10,000 feet in thickness and has been subdivided into three approximately equal portions; the lowest consists of hard, false-bedded coarse, ferruginous, blue sandstones weathering to yellow, reddish and brown, with occasional bands of mottled and blue clay. Above this group lies a succession of mottled clays, blue clays, sandy clays and clayey sandstones with a few considerable beds of hard ferruginous sandstone. Above these clays lies a group of softer blue sandstones containing many fragments of lignite and pebbles of coal and lignite.

(*d*) The most recent of the Tertiary divisions is the Dihing Series, consisting of several thousand feet of pebble beds with subordinate bands of soft clay and sandstone.

7. Above the Tertiary Series are the gravels, sands, and clay forming an "older" alluvium which was laid down when the rivers ran at a much greater elevation than they now do. Some of these beds occur as much as 1,000 feet above the present streams. Lastly, there are the pebble banks, sands and sandy clays now being deposited in the lower reaches of the numerous streams.

8. *Correlation of the Tertiary rocks.*—One of the most remarkable features of the thousands of feet of Assam Tertiaries is the almost complete absence of fossils. The only Tertiary fossils known in the Frontier Tracts are badly preserved leaf impressions and fragments of fossil wood. It is therefore from lithological comparisons with other areas that it is concluded that the Disang Series is mainly Lower Tertiary, that the Coal Measure and Tipam Series are Middle Tertiary, and that the Dihing Series is Upper Tertiary. The total thickness of Tertiary rocks exceeds 30,000 feet and may be as much as 40,000 feet.

STRUCTURAL FEATURES.

9. Having reviewed the sequence of strata found in the Sadiya Frontier Tracts, it is now convenient to consider the characteristics of the four areas mentioned above.

(*a*) *The Hill Country North-West and North of Sadiya.*

10. The eastern continuation of the Himalayas, inhabited by the Miris, Abors, Mishmis, etc., has been very little examined by

geologists; the available geological information regarding this part of the area comes from the work done by the Geological Survey of India. Maclaren in Volume XXXI of the Records of the Geological Survey of India writes "These ranges are, without exception, inhabited by wild hill tribes, whose open or covert hostility, superadded to the difficulty of obtaining transport and the natural inhospitality of the mountains, makes a journey into them a matter of great difficulty if not of actual danger. Indeed our limited knowledge of the geology of their interior has been mainly obtained during the progress of punitive expeditions".

11. These hills have a general west-south-west, east-north-east trend and the rocks found therein strike in the same general direction. The newest rocks occur along the south-eastern margin of the hills and progressively older rocks are found in a north-westerly direction. Throughout the area the first belt of rocks consists of steeply dipping sandstones and conglomerates of Tertiary age which have not been investigated in detail, but which doubtless belong to the Tipam and Dihing Series. Such Tertiary rocks occur in a long belt throughout the Himalayas and they are well-known further west as the Siwalik Series. North-west of and parallel to the Tertiary rocks there is a narrow belt of the Gondwana Series. These rocks have been greatly crushed by the various movements of the earth's crust which have resulted in the uplift of the Himalayas, and in consequence the coal is now found only in very badly crushed lenticles instead of in continuous seams. The series as a whole dips at a high inclination towards the north-west but there are many local variations due to the complications of the folding movements. Still further north-west lies a very great thickness of the metamorphic rocks.

(b) *The Hills East of Sadiya.*

12. The second area includes the high ranges lying across the head of the Assam Valley. The trend of the ranges, and of the beds of rock composing them is at right angles to the direction of the hills referred to in the previous section. The hills at the head of the Valley (*i.e.*, east of Brahmakund) have, like the ranges previously mentioned, been but little examined by Geologists. From Maclaren's summary of the available information (Records of the Geological Survey of India, Volume XXXI) it is seen that, as far as is known, these hills consist entirely of the metamorphic rocks and that the prevalent dip is vertical with a northwest-south east strike. Near Brahmakund are schists, quartzites, and limestone, further south near Daphabum is a large area of gneiss.

(c)—*The Hill Ranges South-East of Sadiya.*

13. The Manabum, Miaobum, Nunnunbum and Patkai ranges and the adjoining valleys of the Dihing and Namphuk have been examined in more detail than the rest of the Frontier Tracts. The area has been referred to in several Geological Survey of India publications but more detailed information regarding these hills has been gathered by the exploratory geological surveys of the Assam Oil Company.

14. In this group of hill ranges the older rocks (Metamorphic and Gondwana) do not appear at the surface, and the hills are composed entirely of Tertiary rocks.

15. *Topography.*—Although the hills are not comparable in height to those of the two ranges already mentioned, the Tertiary outcrop includes areas of very considerable relief, and it is noticeable that the various rock groups have an important bearing on the topography of the country. The more shaly portions of the Disang Series usually occupy low ground but the harder flaggy sandstones stand out as prominent hill ranges. The Coal Measure Series generally occupies comparatively high ground although, owing to the complicated structure of the Coal Measure areas, well defined ridges are seldom noticeable. The sandstones in the lowest portion of the Tipam Series form very prominent hill ranges; small streams crossing the outcrop have to cut their way through the hard sandstones and this usually results in a considerable series of waterfalls and ravines. In the larger streams these sandstones invariably form gorges with steep sides and deep pools. The overlying clays give rise to comparatively low-lying country, which from the neighbouring sandstone ranges appears nearly flat, but which is nevertheless greatly broken by low steep ridges caused by the superior resistance of the sandstone beds to weathering. The sandstones forming the uppermost part of the Tipam Series are comparatively soft but occur in hills of considerable height between Manabum and the Dihing. The outcrop of the Dihing Series is generally marked by low broken hills in which cliffs formed by the pebble beds are common.

16. *Structure.*—The outcrop of Tertiary rocks may, from a structural point of view, be divided into three portions.

17. (*i*) The Patkai range is a scarp of various sandstone beds near the base of the Coal Measures and in the Disang Series, and throughout a large area near the Patkais the rocks have a general west-south-west, east-north-east strike. The Nongyong Valley on the south side of the Patkais is occupied by a syncline in Coal Measures. The broken ground immediately to the north of the Patkais including the Honkapbum and Nunnunbum ranges and extending north-east to the confluence of the Nam Dapha contains rocks of all the Tertiary divisions except the Dihings

and the structure although conforming in general to the west south-west, east-north-east trend, is decidedly complex. A series of strike faults have been identified running approximately parallel to the Patkai range. These faults are accompanied by a considerable amount of contortion specially in the Disang and Coal Measure Series and this line of disturbance represents the continuation of the Disang Thrust Fault of the Naga Hills. The rocks dip at very high angles, being usually vertical or somewhat inverted and their strike, although variable, is more or less parallel to the Patkais.

18. (*ii*) The rocks occurring in the hills to the north-east of the Noa Dihing (the Manabum Range) and in the upper reaches of the Nam Dapha do not show any signs of the west-south-west, east-north-east structural lines, but have a north-north-west, south-south-east strike which is nearly parallel to the direction of folding shown in the Miju and other ranges east of Brahmakund. In the area from the Tenga Pani to the Noa Dihing the lower divisions of the Tertiary rocks lie at a considerable depth below the surface and only the Dihing Series and the uppermost part of the Tipam Series are to be found outcropping.

19. (*iii*) Besides these two areas in which the structure conforms to well marked lines of folding, there is an intervening area including most of the Miaobum range where the rocks have felt the effect of both systems of folding and accordingly exhibit most complex structure. In this area occur both Coal Measures and Tipams, but the dips vary from horizontal to vertical and conform to no general direction, and it is evident that the rocks have been severely folded and also considerably faulted.

(*d*) *Low ground near Sadiya.*

20. The remaining portion of the Sadiya Frontier Tract is the low ground bordering the Dihang, Dibang, Lohit and Noa Dihing rivers. This stretch of country is entirely composed of alluvial deposits brought down from the hills by the large rivers. This alluvium forms a complete mask entirely concealing the geological structure but we may surmise that there is a large synclinal area between the opposing lines of uplift of the Patkais and the Himalayas. It is believed that the alluvium reaches a vast thickness probably measurable in thousands of feet, occupying a depression which has been slowly growing in depth ever since the time of the great Himalayan earth movements, a growth which is probably still continuing. The high level terraces of river gravel, already mentioned as occurring at heights up to as much as one thousand feet above the level of the valley, are found near the head of the Diyun (Dihing), and near Nizamghat on the Dibang and Pasighat on the Dihang.

GEOLOGICAL HISTORY.

21. The Sadiya Frontier Tract does not form an isolated geological unit and its past history can be deciphered only by reference to other areas of which the geology is better known. A chapter on the "Past History of the Himalayan Area" is included in the Memoir by Colonel Burrard and Sir Henry Hayden.

22. It seems likely that the old Metamorphic rocks were deposited on the bed of a considerable sea which covered most of what is now India. The subsequent history of the Frontier Tract is quite unknown until the much later Gondwana period is reached; at that time a large sea or ocean (known to geologists as the Tethys) occupied the present Tibet as well as other countries to the east and to the west. The southern shore of this sea probably lay in a more or less east and west line passing through or near to the Sadiya Frontier Tract and to the south lay a very large continent (known as Gondwana-land) extending over much of Australia, India, and Africa. There was considerable volcanic activity near the coast line of the old Tethys sea and the Abor basalts are lava flows from these old volcanoes; it may be surmised that for a fairly long time there existed in the northern part of the Gondwana-land marshy coastal plains which were covered with vegetation from which were derived the coal seams of Damuda age.

23. After the period of deposition of these early coal-bearing rocks there is another great break in the history of the area but it can be surmised that most of the Frontier Tract continued as part of the continent of Gondwana-land. Just before the Tertiary period as a result of subsidences of the earth's crust this great continent began to break up and the sea commenced an advance in a north-easterly direction towards Upper Assam, eventually submerging a great part, possibly all, of the present Sadiya Frontier Tract. A large area—including the present sites of the Himalayas, the Assam Valley and the Naga Hills—received a great thickness of shallow water deposits and during a long period this area was almost continously sinking. The deposits were probably derived from land to the north which was uplifted during the commencement of the folding movements which gave rise to the Himalayan ranges. During most of this period abundant vegetation grew in swampy areas within or bordering upon the gulf or estuary which had its head somewhere near the northern portion of the Sadiya Frontier Tract. Later in the Tertiary period the gulf became almost entirely silted up and the continuation of the mountain building movements resulted in the formation of the great hill ranges of the Himalayas and Patkais separated by a deep depression. Since their original uplift these ranges have been subjected to intense denudation.

24. The Sadiya Frontier Tract contains evidence of the very recent age of the great folding and mountain building movements that were responsible for the uplift of the Himalayas. Although the age of the Dihing Series cannot be precisely ascertained, its occurrence at inclinations up to 85° and 90° and the absence of evidence of widespread discordance amongst the various Tertiary rock series show that much of the folding must have taken place in very late Tertiary times. From the evidence of high level alluvial deposits and the steep gradient of such streams as the Dihang and Dibang it seems likely that uplift is still in progress or has only quite recently ceased.

ECONOMIC GEOLOGY.

25. *Coal.*—Coal occurs in two separate Geological Series. The older (Gondwana) coal has been so badly crushed by the mountain building movements that the outcrops in the Frontier Tracts have no commercial value. The newer coal seams are found in the upper portion of the Coal Measure Series of the Tertiary and these are being worked in the adjacent Lakhimpur district. The seams in the Frontier Tracts are, however, much thinner; they outcrop in the Miaobum and Nunnunbum Ranges, but are found dipping at very high angles (80° for example) and are somewhat crushed and faulted. It does not seem at all likely that coal could at present be successfully extracted on a commercial scale.

26. *Oil.*—Oil is obtained on a commercial scale from the Tertiary rocks in the neighbouring Lakhimpur district and there is evidence of oil and gas in the Dihing Valley and the Nunnunbum range associated with rocks of the Coal Measure Series. Owing to the steeply folded and greatly faulted condition of the strata there seems no possibility whatever of any appreciable accummulation of oil having taken place and no areas have been found sufficiently promising for even a trial boring.

27. *Gold.*—The gravels of many of the rivers contain minute quantities of gold. The proportion is greatest in the Subansiri, but even here the amount is so small that it is unlikely that its extraction could be made a paying proposition. This gold is presumably obtained from gold-bearing quartz veins occurring amongst the metamorphic rocks somewhere in the hills, but the locality is quite unknown.

28. *Other metals.*—Copper, lead, silver and iron have all been obtained by the Khamtis from the metamorphic rocks occurring in the hills east of Brahmakund, but there is no evidence available of any large occurrences of these ores. In any case th inaccessibility of the country would make working very difficult.

29. *Lime.*—Considerable quantities of lime have been obtained by collecting and burning the limestone boulders brought down by several of the streams.

Other Minerals.—*Sand* and *road metal* are also obtainable from the stream beds. Good *clay* is unlikely to be found in great quantity owing to the admixture of sand.

BIBLIOGRAPHY.

31. The following are the recent references to the geology of the Sadiya Frontier Tract :—

(*a*) Records, Geological Survey of India, Volume XXXI (1904), J. H. Maclaren.

(*b*) A Sketch of the Geography and Geology of the Himalayan Mountains and Tibet by Colonel Burrard and Sir Henry Hayden, Part 4 (1908).

(*c*) Records, Geological Survey of India, Volume XIII (1912), J. Coggin Brown (Geological Results of Abor Expedition).

(*d*) Memoirs, Geological Survey of India, Volume XL, Part 2 (1914), Dr. Pascoe (Petroleum Occurrences of Assam and Bengal).

The above papers contain full references to the earlier work of La Touche and others and to various observations made in the hills further west.

ANNEXURE B.

1. *The copper temple and ruins of Bhishmaknagar near Sadiya.*—The Copper Temple stands in the south-western section of a rectangular area enclosed by a brick wall, measuring 218 by 139 feet. The temple itself is a square of a little over 10 feet only. It cannot have been the main building inside this area and the brick wall evidently enclosed some sort of a palace or fort, the other buildings of which have disappeared. The name is explained by a tradition which says that the temple originally was covered with copper, but no traces of this have been left and the clamps holding the stones of the walls together are all of iron. It seems to me more likely that the image put up in the temple was some form of Durgā, called Tāmres' vari, and that the story of the temple being covered with copper originated from a misunderstanding of that name. The place is now called Tāmresarī, which evidently represents the modern pronunciation of the Sanskrit word Tāmres' vari.

D. Blockh's account of the Copper Temple in 1904-05.

In its present state, the temple is nothing more than a heap of broken stones, with only a part of the walls standing. The roof has gone entirely, and a huge tree grows over the debris. The building is past all repairs; evidently there was very little carving on the stone walls except on the lintel and the jambs of the door, which was in the northern wall. The two figures on the lintels are images of Mahadeva. The roof probably was pyramidal as in similar small temples. The stones of the temple are of pale-pink and greyish-green colour. I chipped off two fragments, which Mr. E. Vredenburg of the Geological Survey has been good enough to examine, who wrote to me as follows :—

"The pale-pink coloured one is a fine grained granite and the greyish-green one an impure sandstone. The latter is similar to rocks that are very frequent amongst the newer Tertiary strata that fringe the Himalaya. Rocks of that age have been mapped to the north of Sadiya. The granite might have been obtained from the same neighbourhood a little further within the hill ranges, or, still more probably, from boulders washed down in streams or contained in the alluvial terraces that are frequent along the banks of the tributaries of the Brahmaputra. This may have been, indeed, the immediate origin of both kinds of rock. East of Sadiya the metamorphic rocks which probably contain granites, extend right up to the border of the plain without the intervention of any Tertiary strata."

A few lines of brick walls are seen to the north of the Copper Temple.

The large enclosure wall is built of very fine bricks similar to those used in the gate and walls of Dimapur city, which again in fabric are very much like the bricks used in the old Muhammadan buildings in Bengal. The thickness of the wall is 3 feet. The gate is in the northern side. Inside three faces of the wall, except the eastern one, had a line of carved tiles about three feet distance from each other. They measure on the average 11 by 13 inches, with a thickness of one inch. All the specimens which I recovered have been photographed. Of these 12 were still *in situ*, but taken out by me to have them cleaned and photographed; the remaining four were dug out from the debris. The total number of tiles must have been more than a hundred, when the wall was complete, and it might be possible to recover a few more, as the spaces, where the tiles were placed into the wall, still can be seen. I could only devote a few hours to this digging, and the men had to use bamboos, no spades being available. It seems, however, very unlikely that any more complete specimens will be found, as the bricks subsequently fallen down generally must have smashed them to pieces. Thus of one tile with the figure of a cock on it, not more than five fragments making up only half of the original could be found despite of careful searching. The tiles have been placed by me inside the Copper Temple, but I think it would be better to have them removed to some Museum, where they could easily be seen.

The carvings represent figures of men, animals, birds, flowers and geometrical patterns, evidently without any symbolic meaning attached to them, whether religious or otherwise. The style is of the semi-barbarian kind, as in the carving at Dimapur and other places in Assam. As instances of this, I refer to the figures of a tiger or lion, which is very similar in treatment to the figures of a lion mounting on an elephant, seen on the broken V columns from Dimapur. The type of course is Indian and only too common in *mediæval* Indian art, but the design, especially of the mane and tail in the Assam figures, is peculiar. The peacock of which two are represented on another tile with their bodies twisted around each other, is also a favourite device on the Dimapur columns, and the ornamental pattern of the tile No. 7 in the following list occurs again on some of the V columns in the newly discovered third group of pillars at Dimapur, with which I shall deal later on. The following is a list of the carvings represented on the tiles :—

(1) bearded man, dancing, holding staff in right hand, and unknown object in uplifted left hand;

(2) beardless man with conical cap, running, spear in right hand; dagger fastened to left side of girdle;

(3) pair of dancers; their uplifted right hands hold some sort of musical instrument (?), the left hands holding a stick rest on the hip; perforated ears; eyes and mouths wide opened, stump noses and hair arranged in strains ending in spirals;

(4) two peacocks with their bodies twisted around each other; small tree or flower on each side;

(5) lion or tiger standing against tree with forelegs uplifted, tongue protruding from its mouth; tail ending in a cluster of five bunches of hair;

(6) horse with saddle and bridle;

(7) circle formed by two lines with dots between; inside ornament formed by twisting a rope or chord into four larger and many smaller irregular circles or ellipses;

(8) plant with five long pointed leaves;

(9) two squares laid crosswise into each other; corners filled with ornamental springs; in inner square ornamental flower with four small and four large petals;

(10) group of four flowers; largest cup-shaped with four leaves or petals on each side; two small flowers below and an unblossomed bud rising over largest flower:

(11) lotus-shaped ornament with eight petals arranged around circle in centre, having cluster of nine drops;

(12) falcon carrying heron;

(13) dancing figure; right hand uplifted, left hand resting on hip; head resembles those of dancers on tile No. 3; tile broken;

(14) five fragments making up half the original tile, which evidently had a bird resembling a cock as ornament;

(15) fabulous bird with pointed crest; I am unable to suggest what kind of bird this means; two pieces corner missing;

(16) three pieces; lotus-shaped ornament similar to that in tile No. 11, in circle formed by two lines.

A further link connecting these ruins with the remains at Dimapur consists in the base and capital of a stone pillar, which, when complete, seems to have been similar to the so-called chessman-columns at that place. They were found in the north-eastern section of the enclosed area. I found two such bases, their shape is octagonal, 2 feet 6 inches in diameter, with a circular hollow inside; these rested on squares, with their corners cut off and differently moulded. The hemispherical capital measures 2 feet 4 inches in diameter at its base and is perforated by a hollow shaft 1 foot 10 inches long. Near the bottom a pair of snakes biting their tails is twisted around it and hold four irregular shaped bolts or knots projecting from the round surface.

East of the enclosure wall are some more ruins of brick and stone buildings. Among those I found three statues of Hindu deities. Two of them could easily be recognised as images of Surya and of Kali dancing on Siva, while the third probably represents Sarasvati, if the indistinct object, which she holds in her right hand, is a musical instrument, as I am inclined to think.

It is impossible in the absence of any inscriptions or traditions to determine the age of these remains. I found only one mark on one of the stones of the Copper temple, which may be read as the letter ja, but even then that particular form of the letter has been in use for several centuries and no historical conclusions can be based upon such slender palæographical evidence.

The ancient city of Bhishmaknagar had to be left unexplored by me. The task of cleaning the thick undergrowth that now covers the area would have been very costly apart from the difficulty of getting labour up there. Only a small path for the elephants has been cut through the jungle, by which I approached the eastern rampart and ditch which surrounded the city, and which I followed up for a distance of about one mile. It is impossible at present to estimate the extent of the city. Its area may cover several square miles. No rumour has yet come forth of the existence of any remains of buildings inside this enormous tract. The Mishmis, who get about hunting there, say that nothing is to be found in the jungle. Until some definite reports of ruins likely to be discovered inside the city enclosure has been received, I do not think that it would be justified to incur the large expenditure of clearing the jungle, which would cost several thousands of rupees, even if it will be possible to induce labourers to work there for a month or two.

ANNEXURE C.

Captain Kingdon Ward, Indian Army Reserve of Officers, the well known traveller and botanist, accompanied by Earl Cawdor left Kalimpong in March 1924 for Southern Tibet *vid* the Karo La and Lhassa Road to the Tsangpo and downstream to Tsetang: thence they continued on Bailey and Morshead's route to Tsela Dzong, except that at Trap, two days below Tsetang, they were compelled to make a 3 days' 'detour' to the north through Osa Dzong and over the Lung La: Bailey had turned southwards here on his journey upstream in 1923. In June 1924 they crossed the Tsangpo and ascended the Doshung La, which is on the main Himalayan Divide and on the South of the Tsangpo and which was crossed by the members of the Abor Survey Party in 1913. They had hoped to visit Pemakoi and to examine the bend of the Tsangpo. Failing to do so owing to the rains, they had to turn back and summer at Tumbatse.

In October 1924 they again crossed the Doshung La into the unadministered area of the Sadiya Frontier Tract and visited Pemakoi. Returning to Gyala, they left on 16th November 1924 for the descent of the Tsangpo to Gompo Ne on the part of the river not traced by Bailey and Morshead in 1913. After five days marches they reached Pemakoi-chung, and after another eight days, the narrowest part of the gorge with sheer cliffs hundreds of feet high on either side. They were compelled to climb out and that evening Ward found the course of the Tsangpo broken by a waterfall of some 40 feet which he described as the "rainbow fall". He was unable to approach nearer than 600 yards.

On December 2nd, 1924, they crossed the Ridge within the great bend of the Tsangpo and descended to Payi. Two further marches brought them to a rope bridge, 3 miles below the Po-Tsangpo confluence by which they crossed and continued to Gompo Ne. The river bed at the rope-bridge was found by boiling point to be 2,239 feet below its level at the 'rainbow' fall. Leaving Gompo Ne they crossed the Po-Tsangpo and ascended the Tsangpo. After 2 miles they were stopped by sheer cliffs which the Mönbas said were impossible. They found a way to climb out and on the second day from the crest of a ridge saw a long stretch of the river 4,000 feet below. Captain Ward descended to the river bed in search of the reported falls. Here he found the river rushing through a narrow gorge with a fall of at least 100 feet in a quarter of a mile. At one point its course was interrupted by a ledge of rock through a 10 foot breach in which the water foamed. Above this ledge there were furious rapids—in 100 yards the river appeared to fall 60 feet and below there was another vertical fall. Captain Ward did not succeed in reaching this. On his return he was able to fix two conspicuous cliffs above the falls and he was able to put in the course of the river round the big bend. With these details Captain Ward has removed the age-old mystery of the Tsangpo falls and endorsed Captain Bailey's work on the Tsangpo gorge. (With acknowledgments to Captain Ward and the Royal Geographical Society.)

Note.—Captain Ward has published his experiences 'The Riddle of the Tsangpo Gorges' (Arnold, London).

GAZETTEER.

AIYENG.—Padam (Abor) village above the right bank of the Dihong river opposite Pasighat (5 miles).

BISA.—A small village on the Kharem stream, two miles above its junction with the Buri Dihing, the residence of Jowhing Chesan, representative descendant of the Bisa clan to whom there is frequent reference in frontier history.

BURI DIHING or Namphuk river rises on the northern slopes of the Patkoi range, which it drains, flows eastward and for a portion of its course forms part of the southern boundary of the Sadiya Frontier Tract. It pursues a tortuous course to divide Lakhimpur and Sibsagar districts and joins the Brahmaputra some 30 miles below Dibrugarh. It is crossed by a Railway bridge at Margherita headquarters of the Assam Railways and Trading Company, Limited. Up to 40 years ago, this river carried off most of the water of the present Noa Dihing river but attempts by the Singphoes of the Noa Dihing basin to improve their stream diverted a large quantity of the stream to form the present Noa Dihing river, a fair sized stream liable to heavy floods which enters the Lohit-Brahmaputra on the left bank, 10 miles upstream of Sadiya. This diversion was probably a contributary cause of the erosion at Sadiya.

BOMJUR.—Formerly an outpost site and now a halting stage on the Sadiya-Nizamghat road, 22 miles from Sadiya on the left bank of the Dibong adjacent to the Mishmi hamlet Bomjur. The Abor village of Bomjur is on the right bank of the Dibong, three miles upstream. No accommodation.

CHOUKHAM.—The principal Khamti village and residence of Raja Chowna Khamti,* the leading member of his tribe in Assam, situated at the junction of the Te-eng-Bereng (Kamlung) 86 miles by boat from Sadiya, *viâ* Noa Dehingmukh and Tengapani. There

*Died 3rd July 1935.

is a cold weather route by road to Dikarumukh (35 miles from Sadiya, thence 2½ miles, *vid* Namphai (Bhetagaon), a village on the Bereng (Tengapani). A small bazar, few supplies including paddy, no accommodation. There is an opium shop at Choukham.

DAMBUK.—The main Padam (Abor) village, 300 houses, in the Sadiya Tract offshoot of Damroh the parent Padam village. Route (1) 7 miles from Nizamghat, crossing the Dibong ½ mile below the stockade, (2) crossing Dibong to Abor-Bomjur, from Bomjur and thence 8 miles by track. No supplies, no accommodation.

DENNING.—The main stage on the Lohit Valley Road, 70 miles from Sadiya. There is an outpost of Assam Rifles and a Dispensary, route 6 stages. Inspection Bungalows furnished; no attendance or *vid* Digarumukh, Tezumukh and Upper Teju (32 miles) cart road.

DEOPANI.—The name of a river which rises in the hills east of Nizamghat and flows southwards parallel and close to the Dibong and the Sadiya-Nizamghat road which it crosses at mile 5½, it is bridged there in the cold weather. In the vicinity of mile 5½—7 are several ancient tanks—with bricked sides and not inconsiderable bunds, etc.; known to the Abor and Miris as Jitarang.

HAKATI.—A village and stream, which for portion of its course forms part of the boundary between Sadiya and the Saikhoa mauza of Lakhimpur. There is a tea garden being opened out in the vicinity of the village: east of Saikhoaghat 7 miles surface cart tract.

KOBO.—River base for Pasighat situated on the river bank of the Brahmaputra one mile below the Lalle confluence—20 miles down stream of Saikhoa and 25 miles of Sadiya. From Kobo starts the Kobo-Yembung road, *vid* Pillung (mile 11½) and Pasighat mile 21-22. The cart road which is passable for light motor traffic ends at Pasighat. The bridle path to

Yembung continues 33 miles further. From Kobo a surface track takes off to Murkong Selek (7 miles down-stream); Headquarters of the Veneer Mills, Assam Saw Mills and Timber Company, Limited. There is a small guard of the Assam Rifles at Kobo and a combined Post and Telegraph office. Saikhoaghat is railhead for Kobo; there is no regular boat service and boats (dug-outs) have to be arranged at Sadiya or Kobo. The Kobo-Pasighat dâk comes *vid* Saikhoaghat. From May to November the Feeder Service from Dibrugarh to Sadiya serves Kobo. There is a surface road from Saikhoa to the left bank of the Brahmaputra opposite Kobo but ferrying is at present uncertain.

KIRIM.—An Abor village on the Sadiya-Nizamghat road—9 miles from Sadiya. The Kirim stream crosses this road at mile 13 where is the first halting stage to Nizamghat. No accommodation.

KUNDIL.—A river joining the Lohit-Brahmaputra just above Sadiya bazar crossing the Sadiya-Sanpura road on the 2nd mile. Bridged.

LAIMAKURI.—Headquarters of the Meckla Nuddee Tea Box Mills of the Assam Saw Mills and Timber Company, Limited, situated on the Burisuti channel 20 miles on the right bank of the Brahmaputra upstream of Dibrugarh, served at intervals by the Feeder Steamer. Post office and bazar; Company's Dispensary.

MEBO.—A large Padam (Abor) village 3 miles east-south-east of Ayeng overlooking the Sikku stream.

MIMESIPO.—A small Padam village 8 miles west of Dambuk practically a portion of Siluk.

MISHMI.—The general name for the tribes inhabiting the Lohit Valley and the valleys of the Dibong river and its tributaries. In the lower Lohit Valley live the Taroan known as the Digaru Mishmis; in the Upper Lohit Valley the Miju (Miju Mishmis), in the Dibong Valley the Midi (Chulikata or crophairer-Mishmis), in the Ithun Valley (a tributary of the Dibong) the Midu (Bebejiya Mishmis).

MURKONG SELEK.—Headquarters of Veneer Mills, Assam Saw Mills and Timber Company, Limited

Combined Post and Telegraph Office. Forest Range Office, bazar. There is a Forest rest house, small bazar, few supplies. Route, *viâ* Kobo river and surface cart road (7 miles) or *viâ* Dibrugarh (Feeder Steamer) at irregular intervals.

NINGRU.—A Singpho village on the right bank of the Noa Dihing river 20 miles above the mouth, where lives Moria Somoan, decendant of the Ningru frontier history. There is a Khamti village also at Ningru. An opium shop, few supplies. No accommodation.

NOADIHING or the DIYUN river rising on the northern slopes of the Chookan mountains in the extreme east-south-east corner of the district flows through the area occupied by the Singphoes and joins the Lohit-Brahmaputra (about 10 miles east of Sadiya). Ordinarily a large portion of its water finds its way down the Buridihing by the Margantuan and Khaikhe channels below Maiyo.

NIZAMGHAT situated on the Dibong at the end of the Sadiya-Nizamghat cart road (34 miles) (cold weather, passable for motor traffic) due north of Sadiya where the Dibong river emerges from the hills A cold weather outpost of Assam Rifles. No supplies No accommodation.

PARSURAMKUND.—Where the Lohit Brahmaputra emerges from the hills, a place of pilgrimage for Hindus. Route—cart road cold weather from Sadiya, *viâ* Sunpura (15 miles, Serai, few supplies), Digarumukh 25½ miles—no accommodation, no supplies. Tezumukh (37½ miles), no accommodation, no supplies. Temei 46½ mile, serai, no supplies. Crossing the Lohit-Brahmaputra at Temei by a Mishmi Ferry a path leads to the Kund 4 miles further; two serais, no supplies.

PASIGHAT.—Headquarters of the Pasighat subdivision on the right bank of the Dihong river, Assistant Political Officer and Abor Outposts, of combined Post and Telegraph Office, Charitable Dispensary, 21 miles from Kobo by cart road passable for motor traffic, *viâ* Pillung 11½ miles. There are furnished inspection bungalows at Kobo, Pillung, Pasighat, no attendance, few supplies. Small bazar at Kobo and Pasighat.

SADIYA.—Headquarters of the Sadiya Frontier Tract district. Usual district offices. Headquarters of the 2nd (Lakhimpur) Battalion, Assam Rifles, Charitable Dispensary, combined Post and Telegraph Office, Divisional Sub-Treasury, good bazar. Inspection bungalow. No Dâk Bungalow but visitors are permitted to occupy the inspection bungalow. No attendance. Sadiya is situated on the right bank of the Lohit-Brahmaputra, 6 miles from Saikhoaghat (rail-head) terminus of the Dibru-Sadiya Railway situated on the left bank of the Lohit. Route to Saikhoa by dug-out ferry system across the sands in the cold weather. Boats can be arranged in advance from Sadiya if notice is given. The Sadiya bazars are thronged in the cold weather with strange primitive peoples from the mountains.

SAIKHOAGHAT.—Terminus of the Dibru-Sadiya Railway for Sadiya, Kobo, Pasighat, Murkong Selek. Combined Post and Telegraph office. Inspection Bungalow and Dâk Bungalow furnished. No attendance.

SANPURA.—Terminus of the Lohit Valley and Sunpura, Temei, Parsuramkund roads. On the Balijan river left bank 15 miles from Sadiya—cart road—motorable. Charitable Dispensary, Inspection Bungalow, no attendance, no supplies.

SILLUK.—Padam village of 100 houses between Dambuk and Mebo everlooking Sibia stream.

INDEX.

A

B

C

E

F

M

N

BALIPARA FRONTIER TRACT GAZETTEER.

PART II.

CONTENTS.

BALIPARA FRONTIER TRACT.

THE BALIPARA FRONTIER TRACT.

The Balipara Frontier Tract is bounded on the north by Bhutan, Tibet and the hills inhabited by the Mombas of Rupa and Shergaon, the Akas, Daflas, Apa Tanangs and Hill Miris ; on the west it is bounded by the district of Kamrup and on the south and east by the districts of Darrang and Lakhimpur. Physical aspects.

From the plains there are a considerable number of passes into the hills, the principal being the Udalguri-Amratulla trade route into Tibet; this is actually the shortest route between India and Lhassa, the distance being 311 miles, against 350 by the Chumbi Valley route. This road is good excepting for the first 25 miles.

Other passes west of the Bhoreli are the Doimara-Rupa and Doimara-Shergaon routes, and the Charduar-Bhalukpung route into the Aka Hills. The passes from Doimara are easy and practical for pack animals. East of the Bhoreli there are many routes leading into the hills. They are difficult and only fit for coolie transport.

Many rivers drain the hills on this portion of the Frontier. The two largest are the Subansiri and the Bhoreli, both of which break through the main snow range to the north having their sources in the table lands of Tibet.

Wild animals which are found in the tract are Elephant, Rhinoceros (both unicornis and Sumatrensis), Buffalo (Bos bubalis) Bison or Mithon (Bos gaurus and Bos frontalis). Of deer, are found the Sambhar, Hog deer, Chital, Swamp, Musk, and Barking deer. Of goats, the Serow and Gurral, and in the further hills the Takin (Budorcas taxicolor). The tiger, leopard, clouded leopard, sloth bear, binturong, pig, pigmy hog, the wild dog, and many kinds of cats. Wild animals.

History. The southern portion of the tract originally formed part of the districts of Darrang and Lakhimpur and the early history of this portion will be found in the Gazetteer of these districts. In 1914, the Western Section, North-East Frontier, was formed into a district under the control of a Political Officer.

Monyúl meaning in Tibetan " The low country " is a name applied to the portion of the North-East Frontier about 2,000 square miles in extent, which is wedged in between Bhutan on the west and the Miji and Aka Hills on the east. It is divided from Tibet proper by a wild range of mountains averaging 16,000 feet.

The people inhabiting this area are called by the Tibetans Mombas, *i e*, inhabitants of the Monyül (low country).

Inhabitants. The inhabitants of the triangle south of the Sela Range are divided loosely into two main tribes, *viz.*, Sherchokpa and Sherdukpen.

Mombas. The Sherchokpa live in the valley of the Dirang Chu as far as the village of Rahung and of the Nagum Chu (Dhansiri river) ; the Sherdukpen are the inhabitants of the villages of Shergaon and Rupa.

The Mombas north of the Sela are under the administration of the Tsonajong Jongpens one of whom is a monk, the other a layman, appointed by the authorities at Lhassa. In the summer time these two officials live at Tsonajong, in Tibet proper; in the winter time they live at Tawang in the Monyül. Tsonajong is a place of some importance as a trade mart, as here the Assam Trade route is intersected by the Trade route from Eastern Tibet and China.

All revenues collected by the Tsona Jongpens are sent direct to Lhassa.

South of the Sela, the Sherchokpas are under the control of two monk Jongpens appointed by the Tawang monastery, a large monastery of 500 monks, an offshoot of the important Drepung monastery at Lhassa with the exception of the village of Senge Dzong which is under the Tsona Jongpens.

All revenues collected by the monk Jongpens go to the support of the monastery.

The language spoken varies greatly from village to village, but the majority speak a dialect resembling the language spoken in Eastern Bhutan.

These Mombas are a quiet law abiding people amongst whom serious crime is practically unknown, they are excellent farmers, industrious and hard working, and if it were not for the exactions levied by the monks the country would be very prosperous.

The dress of the Momba is distinctive ; he wears a short coarse woollen Chuba or Tibetan Cloak dyed red, which reaches a short way below the hips ; underneath he wears short loose pants of coarse white cotton cloth. His hair is cut short just above the eyes and at the nape of the neck, and on his head he wears a peculiar dome shaped cap of Yak hair with untrimmed edges. In his belt he invariably carries a short stout sword in a wooden scabbard.

The Jongpens of Tsona receive annually a subsidy of Rs. 5,000 from the British Government under Treaty (see Aitchison's Treaties, Part IV, Bhutan No. CVI, Page 267). Of this amount Rs. 500 is kept by the Tawang monastery, and the balance sent to the Drepung monastery at Lhassa.

The Sherdukpen are a small tribe of Mombas, independent of Tawang, and live in the large villages of Shergaon and Rupa. These two villages were formerly called Ruprai Gya and Sur Gya, but from constant dealings with Assam the present form has been adopted. They are quiet peace loving agriculturists and are finer men than the other Mombas living south of the Sela. These two villages are ruled by a joint council of seven headmen, who in the old days were called *Sàt Rajà* by the Assamese. These people are divided into two classes, the upper or the hereditary land holders and a poorer class called Giba. There is no slavery amongst them. They mix little with other Mombas. They migrate to the Plains at Doimara in the Frontier Tracts for five months every year, and bring with them all their live stock consisting of ponies, mules and a very fine handsome breed of cattle.

They received from us a yearly subsidy of Rs. 2,526-7-0, and consider themselves under the protection of the British Raj.

The Tembang, Konia and But Mombas were called in the past "the Thebengia Bhutias" by the Assamese. Their villages are situated about 25 miles north of Rupa, on a fertile undulating plateau at an altitude of 6,000 feet; they are a miserable, degraded people, being much ground down by the Mijis who are their immediate neighbours. In spite of this they are hard working and if only they could obtain some measure of protection might become a prosperous community. These villages are independent of Tawang. They receive from us annually the sum of Rs. 145-13-6 as *Posa*.

The Mombas are Buddhists and in most of their villages is a Gompa (temple) and to judge from outward signs they should be good Buddhists for on every corner of the road one finds a "Mane" wall or Chorten and in the neighbourhood of each village every stream is used to turn a huge prayer wheel. Their Buddhism, however, is very superficial; in the few villages that have priests these have succumbed to the world the flesh and the devil and taken unto themselves wives thus *ipso facto* renouncing their holy orders. They however continue to perform their office though they have long lost the respect of their flocks.

The Akas. The Akas inhabit the Tenga, Digien, and lower part of the Bichom river valleys.

The word 'Aka' means in Assamese painted, the Tibetan name for these people is Khanchh or Black lips, both names are due to the Aka habit of smearing their lips and cheeks with a black resinous substance derived from the Blue pine (*Pinus Excelsa*) as a protection against biting flies and blistering winds.

The Akas call themselves Hrusso. They claim descent from two chiefs, Notapur and Bayu, who in ancient times lived in the stone forts at Bhalukpung on the Bhoreli river. The remains of these forts are still to be seen.

Though a small tribe the Akas are superior in education and civilization to their neighbours and are held in high esteem by them.

Their history.

Practically nothing is known of the history of the Akas before the British occupation. The British first came in contact with the tribe in 1829 when the depredations of Tagi, the Kovatsun chief, necessitated action being taken against them. Tagi was arrested and confined for four years in the Gauhati Gaol. Immediately on release he took again to his old habits of raiding which culminated in the capture and massacre of a small military outpost at Balipara in 1835. A price was placed on his head but no expedition was made into the Hills. In 1841 he twice raided and carried off British subjects into the hills. On this the Government half-heartedly gave sanction for an expedition against him, but whilst preparations were being made he came in and surrendered. He was forgiven, on condition of his swearing allegiance and a pension of Rs. 240 was bestowed on him, in 1844 this pension was increased to Rs. 360 per annum and again was increased to Rs. 520 in 1848.

The Akas gave no further trouble until 1883. This year was the year of the Calcutta Exhibition, and specimens of agricultural inplements and products, wearing apparel, ornaments and weapons of Frontier tribes were wanted for exhibit. The Mauzadar of Balipara was sent up with 18 followers by the Government to try to procure these articles, and if possible to obtain an Aka man and woman for the purpose of modelling. The request was made in a manner that so incensed the Aka Chief that he seized the Mauzadar and his servant and confined them, but allowed the other 12 to go free. At the same time the Kutson chief Medhi, raided the Forest Outpost near Balipara and carried off a Ranger and Clerk.

It was decided to send an Expedition and a mixed force of 970 men including two mountain guns entered the Aka hills in the cold weather of 1884. The advance guard of 150 men was attacked and held up at Tenga river and two men were killed and seven wounded; the main body then came up, the passage of the river was forced, the Akas retreated and the Kovatsun village was occupied; the Akas however retired from their villages and hid themselves in the jungle. When with great difficulty communications were established, it was learned that the mauzadar was dead; the two forest officials were released and some muskets and bayonets captured at Balipara and two rifles taken at Tenga river were given up.

Our casualties were 4 men killed and seven wounded; the Akas suffered no casualties.

The force did not remain in the hills long enough to impress the people but retired almost immediately without imposing any fine, or burning any village. A half-hearted blockade of the Frontier was kept up till 1888 when the Akas came in and on professing submission were pardoned.

Since 1888 the Akas have been well behaved.

In 1913-14 their country was visited by the Political Officer, Western Section, North-East Frontier, the most peaceful relations were established there and the surrounding countries were mapped and explored.

Organization. The Akas are divided into the following clans:—

1. Kutson.
2. Kovatsun.
3. Karam.
4. Golu.
5. Nyobin.
6. Tepun.
7. Pushing.
8. Khosakhyun.
9. Gujeria.
10. Dujia.
11. Miri Aka.

The Akas are the upper class and have under them a class known as Khoas. The Khoas are a distinct community speaking a language of their own; they do most of the manual work of the country, and are paid for their work in kind; they are not in any sense slaves.

The Kutson and Kovatsun are the two most important of the clans. The headquarter village of the former is Jamiri and the latter Gohaintan. The clans live in distinct groups of villages called by the clan name.

The villages are almost invariably built on the healthy sites offered by high flat topped spurs. They are usually small consisting of from 8 to 10 houses.

The Kutson and Kovatsun clans dominate the rest, and in external affairs the heads of these two clans act as Chiefs for the whole country; in dealing with internal affairs they act as presidents of the councils and have no more influence than their personality allows.

Village questions are settled in open council, but those which affect the whole clan or group of clans are settled by a council of village representatives meeting either at Jamiri or at Gohaintan. Every free man has the right of speech, but the method of debate often consists in shouting down dissentients. In cases of doubt lots are cast. Women have considerable influence, but it is exercised behind the scenes as they are not allowed to speak at the village councils.

There is no slavery in the country.

Language.

The Aka language is classified by Grierson as belonging to Tibeto-Burman group but is very difficult to see any resemblance between it and other dialect of the same group.

The Khoa language is entirely distinct from that spoken by the Akas.

Appearance and dress.

The Akas are a well made strongly built race, yellowish brown and of a very Mongolian appearance. They are a platyoprosopic or a flat faced race, their hair is straight and black, the average height of the men is 5′ 4″, of the women under 5′.

A man's dress consists of a short coarse cotton cloth which is wound round the body and pinned over the shoulder by small bamboo pins, the garment is bound round the waist by a *kummerbund* below which it forms a short skirt reaching to a little below the knees. A jacket is worn which reaches to the hips, sometimes this jacket has sleeves, sometimes it is sleeveless; often it is merely a cloth wound round the shoulders.

The hair is twisted into a knot at the top of the head. The head dress is a curious pill box like hat made of split bamboo about four inches deep; in front is worn a bunch of feathers or dried bamboo leaves.

The lobes of ears are pierced, in them the rich wear cylindrical pear shaped silver earrings but the majority wear bamboo tubes.

In his belt the Aka wears a *dao*, he also carries a bow and arrows slung across his back.

An Aka woman's dress consists of a cloth wound round her waist similar to that worn by the man but reaching almost to the ankles. She wears a long jacket usually of Assamese silk. Her hair is done up in a knot at the back of her head and round the upper part of her forehead the well-to-do woman wears a very striking fillet of silver chain work; in her ears she wears earrings similar to those worn by the men, and round her neck innumerable necklaces of coloured beads on which are hung silver Tibetan ornaments.

Both men and women wear cotton cloth gaiters to protect them from the bites of Dam Dim (*Simuleum Indicum*), fastened just below the knee with a string of blue beads.

Their houses are well built wooden structures of dressed timber raised off the ground on piles and roofed with thatch or palm leaves. The beams and joists are carefully squared with an adze and are often roughly curved. **Houses.**

Each house is about 60 yds. long and 8 yds. wide. The houses are divided internally into 4 or 5 rooms with a wide verandah at each end.

The front room is the guest room and in it are usually hung the heads of Mithan and wild animals to show the consequence of the host and his prowess in the chase.

These people occupy the upper valley of the Bichom. Their valley is rich and fertile and could easily support a much greater population than it does. The Mijis are closely akin to the Akas both in appearance and customs the two people constantly inter-marry. The Mijis have no chiefs but each village has its headman who possesses considerable authority within his village. **The Mijis.**

Their language is different to that of the Aka. The Miji trades freely with the Tibetans travelling *viâ.* the Mago pass.

The Miri Akas are a fairly large tribe living on the left bank of the Bichom river and also in the Kovu and Pachuk valleys. They are very closely related to the Aka, but they are a good deal less civilized, and are much dirtier. **The Miri Akas.**

They act as a buffer between the Akas and the Daflas living to the north. They are friendly with both tribes.

The Daflas inhabit the portion of the Himalaya from the Bhoreli river eastward to the Khru river, a tributary of the Subansiri river. They are a very large tribe, they may roughly be divided into two main divisions the YANO (or Yan) and the TAGEN. The meaning of the word Dafla is obscure, it is a name given to these people by the Assamese, it is not used amongst them, they refer to themselves in general terms as Bengni (men), but villages are usually called by the Nebu (khel) name. **The Daflas.**

The Yano or Western Daflas inhabit the Hills from the Tibet border north of the Akas as far as the Boroi river. East of the Boroi river and as far as the Khru River live the Tagen Daflas. The two peoples are very much alike in dress and appearance, but speak different dialects.

The people are well made, plucky and very truculent. They have very independent manners which might often be taken for rudeness by a stranger. They would be very formidable if there was any combination between them. There is however practically none though in the face of a great common danger it is possible that they might make common cause. Every village is a separate community living usually in a state of feud with its neighbours. The size of the village is regulated by the nature of the country; if the cultivable area be large the village may be very large also but as a rule 12 houses is the usual size.

The houses are well built wooden structures built on *changs*, and roofed with thatch or palm leaves; they are very long—sometimes as much as 250 feet—and about 8 yards broad. Each house would contain about 50 souls.

The Daflas are divided into a great number of exogamous Nebus or khels such as Bod, Nabbum, Nitung, Tabba, Taching, Bao, Tao, Tagen and many others.

Appearance. The Daflas are short well formed men of considerable muscular development, with large broad flat faces, high cheek bones, and large mouth. They have no hair on cheeks or chins. Many of the Tagen Daflas tattoo their faces, the western very rarely tattoo.

On the head a cane work helmet with a plume of hornbill feathers is worn. A cloth is worn on the body and tied crossways in front over the arms. The hair is done up in a knot on the forehead, through this knot is thrust a brass pin about nine inches long. The sword is slung round the neck by a belt often decorated with cowrie shells.

A long straight *dao* in a bamboo scabbard, a bow, a quiver full of arrows, many of them iron tipped and covered with concoction of aconite and pigs fat, which forms a very deadly poison. When travelling or raiding they carry a long spear. Arms.

Their method of cultivation is by *jhuming* or felling and burning the forest, it is then picked over and cleaned and the earth stirred with a sharp bamboo. The staple crops are hill rice, maize, millet, jobs tears, tobacco and chillies. Cultivation.

The Dafla hills, taken generally, are a very broken mass of mountains, rugged and difficult; the valleys become larger and the slope easier as the snowy range is approached. There are however some very fertile tracts and here the villages are large and close together. Such are the Khru river, Miri pathar, the Popum river, the Dikrang river and the Ranganadi. This latter river is capable of supporting a very large population as it is open country with large undulating grassy valleys. The Ranganadi is the only known portion of the Dafla hills where terraced rice cultivation exists. The country

The Dafla is by religion an animist. He believes in the good and evil spirits of nature, and is constantly employed in trying to placate the Evil Spirits of the winds, the forest, the mountains, etc. The benign spirits do not trouble him as they are well disposed and need no humouring. In every village there is more than one Nyobu or Deodhai who is constantly consulting omens and sacrificing to appease offended spirits. Omens are taken on all occasions, such as before making a raid, a journey, contracting a marriage, at a birth and a death. Religion.

The Daflas have from the first mention we have of them been known as a clamorous and turbulent people. Of them wrote Mahomed Zazim in the day of Aurungzeb, "The Daflas are entirely independent of the Assam Raja, and whenever they find an opportunity plunder the country contiguous to their mountains." History.

From the beginning of our occupation of Assam the Daflas gave much trouble to our local officers, as in the days of the Assam Rajahs the Daflas were given the right to collect from every ten houses one double cloth, one single cloth, one handkerchief, one *dao*, ten head of horned cattle, and four seers of salt. The Assamese living along the Frontier who were thus taxed paid only Rs. 3 instead of Rs. 9 from each *got* to the Government. The Daflas collected these dues in full and were guilty of many acts of oppression in doing so. This right to collect goods was changed in 1852 to the payment of a settled sum which is in force at the present day under the name of *Posa*.

The original *Posa* paid was as follows :—

		Rs.	a.	p.
From Tezpur Treasury to Charduar and Naodwar Daflas.	...	2,491	0	0
From Lakhimpur Treasury to Charduar Daflas.	...	1,243	0	0
From Lakhimpur Treasury to Banskotta Daflas.	...	392	1	6

The Daflas have constantly given trouble making small raids, most of them against Daflas who had settled in the Plains. These raids caused so much irritation that in 1873 a military force attempted to blockade the Hills in order to prevent any Daflas coming to the Plains. The blockade proving inefficient a military force was sent into the Hills on a punitive expedition. This had the effect of causing the Daflas to keep quiet for a few years.

Since then the Daflas have constantly broken the peace ; details will be found in Mackenzie's North-East Frontier and Captain St. John Michell's reports.

Several expeditions have visited the Hills and the hillmen have now learned that their Hills are not utterly inaccessible to our sepoys as they once believed.

Practically all raids have been against Daflas settled in the plains to avenge, what the hillmen believed to be, very just grievances and with no idea that they were disturbing the peace of the British Raj.

These people inhabit a magnificent plateau some ten miles long and six miles broad laid out in highly cultivated and artificially irrigated terraces well watered by the Kali river, a sluggish stream some 45 to 60 feet in breadth with low alluvial banks. The hills surrounding the valley rise to some 1,500 to 2,000 feet above the level of the Kali river the slopes are covered with fine pine forests. The Apa Tanangs.

The people live in large villages — they may almost be called towns — as Hong, the largest village, contains 2,000 houses.

The men are well made averaging about 5′ 6″. They wear their hair like Daflas done up in front in a knot about the forehead, through this knot is passed a brass pin about 7″ long.

The clothing consists of a cloth worn round the waist and brought up and secured over the shoulders whilst over this is worn a square blanket of blue and red striped cloth fastened by with a loop and buttoned round the neck.

Round the waist is worn a curious contrivance made of thin strips of cane dyed a bright scarlet, the cane is formed into a tail behind about 18″ long.

The women wear a short skirt of coloured cotton and a zouave jacket of like material. Their hair is done up in a knot on the top of their heads. In each nostril they wear a round cylinder of wood about an inch in diameter, which horribly disfigures features that would otherwise be pleasant or even comely.

The Apa Tanang or Ankas (tail), as they are locally called, are peaceful agriculturists ; they live at peace with their neighbours and the size of their villages protects them from outside raids. They have a strong tribal feeling and if attacked they would quickly concentrate in order to avenge themselves.

Their system of irrigation is excellent, the whole valley is under cultivation, the distribution of water is very cleverly managed and shows a high degree of organization.

On the surrounding hills excellent crops of maize, millet, jobs tears, etc., are grown.

Bamboos are cultivated for building purposes and the felling of timber both for building and firewood is carefully regulated. When a block of timber is cut for firewood, the wood is stacked and then issued, as the forests are cut blocks of equal size are aforested. Their plantations being carefully tended and fenced round as a guard against cattle.

The valley is governed by a council of elders who wield considerable authority.

The population is probably about 20,000. They are very well off as they sell their superfluous crops to their surrounding neighbours.

Their language differs very considerably from Dafla or Miri.

They are a peaceful people and have only once, in 1896 given trouble, on this occasion they raided and murdered some Hill Miris settled in the plains who they alleged cheated them. A Military Expedition visited their valley shortly after, since then they have been very peaceful.

The Hill Miris.

The Hill Miris inhabit the Subansiri valley as far as the plains. They must in no way be confounded with the Miris living in the plains of Assam, the latter are descended from men of the Dafla, Hill Miri and Abor tribes who have in times past left the hills and settled in the plains, and have now become a distinct community.

They are divided into several clans, Saraks, Panibotia, Tarbotia and Ghasis.

The Panibotia, Tabotia and Saraks are fine tall men of great mosoular strength, they are better looking and slightly more civilized than their Dafla neighbours.

The Ghasi are a small people and not so oivilized as the other Miris.

The Miri villages average about 20 houses, their houses are built on *changs* anl closely resemble those built by the Daflas.

These people are capable of concentration against a common foe and for that reason they are not raided by their neighbours, and lead a peaceful existence. They are well behaved and have never given us any trouble. We have always been on most friendly terms with them.

The *Posa* of Rs. 2,244-12-8 which we pay them is more perhaps of a charity than any we pay on the North-East Frontier.

Their country was visited in 1911-12 by the Miri Mission.

The Assam Frontier Tracts Regulation, 1880 (II of 1880), was extended to the Balipara Frontier Tract by the Government of India in the Foreign and Political Department's Notification No. 979E.B., dated the 25th September 1914. The Scheduled Districts Act, 1874 (XIV of 1874), was declared to be in force in the tract under section 3, clause (*a*) of the said Act, by Notification No. 4959P., dated the 18th August 1916, of the Chief Commissioner of Assam. The following Acts and Regulations have been extended to the tract under section 5 of the Scheduled Districts Act, 1874 :— Administration.

(1) The Indian Penal Code, 1860 (XLV of 1860).

(2) The Indian Police Act, 1861 (V of 1861).

(3) The Indian Arms Act, 1878 (XI of 1878).

(4) The Agriculturists' Loans Act, 1884 (XII of 1884).

(5) The Assam Land and Revenue Regulation, 1886 (I of 1886), with the exception of sections 3 to 159.

(6) The Assam Forest Regulation, 1891 (VII of 1891).

(7) The Whipping Act, 1909 (IV of 1909).

(8) The Assam Rifles Act, 1920 (Assam Act I of 1920).

(9) The Bengal Eastern Frontier Regulation, 1873 (V of 1873).

(10) The Bengal Eastern Frontier (Amendment) Regulation, 1925 (V of 1925).

The Elephant Preservation Act, 1879 (VI of 1879), was also extended to the tract under section I of the said Act by the Chief Commissioner's Notification No. 5470P., dated the 13th October 1914. Under sections 5 and 5A of the Scheduled Districts Act, 1874, section 144 of the Code of Criminal Procedure, 1898 (Act V of 1898), and sections 22, 23, 38(2) and 40 of the Chin Hills Regution, 1896 (V of 1896), were extended to the tract in restricted and modified form by the Chief Commissioner's Notifications Nos. 4961P. and 4962P., dated the 18th August 1916.

The administration of the tract is vested in the Governor in Council, the Political Officer and the native village authorities or such other officer or officers as the Governor in Council may see fit from time to time to appoint in that behalf. The administration of justice is regulated by special rules drawn up under section 6 of the Scheduled Districts Act, 1874, and published with the Chief Commissioner's Notification No. 6728P., dated the 17th November 1914.

The garrison of the tract consists of a battalion of Assam Rifles with headquarters at Lokra, which is the administrative capital of the tract. This battalion also maintains outposts—some permanent and some

periodic—in the various places both outside and within the tract. A list of the outposts is given below :—

Happy Valley (Shillong)	Permanent.
North Lakhimpur ...	
Udalguri	Periodical.
Dikalmukh ...	
Dikrai	
Darranga	

Gold is found in varying quantities in all the Minerals.
streams on this section of the tract. In the days of the old Assam Rajas, when a large population inhabited most parts of the tract, now relapsed into forest, considerable quantities of gold were extracted from these streams. Nowadays a few *sonaris* carry on small operations from time to time.

There is a good deal of mica in the low hills. Samples have been sent to Calcutta and London, and have been well reported on. Mica of the right quality and in sheets of sufficient size is very valuable, and operations, if carried on, might be very profitable.

Coal exists in large quantities in the foot hills bordering on Bhutan. Samples have been sent to Calcutta ; but the report shows that it is immature and is not of much commercial value.

The trade on this Frontier is chiefly with Tibet. Trade.
The figures for 1924 were approximately :—

Imports—Rs. 75,000.
Exports—Rs.1,10,000.

The Tibetans bring down wool, blankets, ponies chillis, musk, bees-wax and baskets.

The exports across the frontier are mainly rice and salt, cotton cloths, and Assam silks.

It should be borne in mind that the trade route between Udalguri and Lhassa is the shortest route from India, being only 311 miles. This route, if only the first 20 miles through the hills were improved—and the difficulties are not great,—would be at least as easy as the Kalimpong Jelap La route, and the trade that comes down would be enormously increased.

Forests. The fisheries on this frontier are not sold. Licenses are taken out by anglers for fishing on the larger rivers.

Agar and *pipul* are obtained in fair quantities and the *mahals* are sold yearly.

Cane is not available in large quantities, the *mahal* only fetching Rs. 1,500 per annum.

Thatching grass is available in plenty, but the *mahal* is not sold.

The Chaulmugra tree (*Turaktogenos Kurzii*) is fairly common, but no enquiries for its fruit have been made.

There are large areas of forest, most of which is constituted into reserves. The usual type of Assam evergreen forest exists in the plains area. The chief species of trees are :—

Amari (*Amoora Wallichi*), Poma (*Cedrela Toona*), Urium (*Bischofia javanica*), Ajhar (*Lagerstrœmia Flos Reginæ*) Hollook (*Terminalia Myriocarpa*), Bola (*Morus Lævigata*), Jutuli (*Altingia excelsa*) Khokan (*Duabanga Sonneratioides*), etc.

On the hills most magnificent timber exists ; enormous oaks of many kinds are to be found and on the ridges Silver Fir (*Abies Webbiana*) while over the firs ridges are many hundred square miles of *Pinus excelsa* (*Kail*), *Pinus longfoilia* (Chir), *Cupressus torulosa* and other *conifers*. But the difficulty of extraction will for some years militate against the successful working of these forests.

Land Revenue.—There are a few cadastrally surveyed villages transferred to this district from Darrang district, on the readjustment of the boundary between this district and Darrang. The Land Revenue of these villages is paid at the rates in force in the neighbouring villages of Darrang. Land Revenue.

In the plains portion of the tract, some small new villages have been opened up after the constitution of this district. Most of them are settlements of hill Daflas coming down to settle in the plains. These villages are assessed to land revenue, the rates being *basti* Re. 1-4, *rupit* Re. 1 and *faringati* annas 9 per *bigha* per annum.

Poll, house and hoe taxes are not levied from any tribe in the tract either in the hills or in the plains.

There are no tea gardens,' one which was formerly included in the district having been retransferred to Darrang district in May 1925.

The greater part of the plains portion of the Balipara Frontier Tract is covered by reserved forests. There are some forest villages, the land revenue realised from them being credited to the head "Forests."

The Excise administration is carried on under executive orders and the Political Officer is directly under the control of Government. There is only one opium shop in the tract. Opium eaters in the area have been registered and they can obtain opium only on production of their ration tickets. Excise.

The Medical supervision is in the charge of the Civil Surgeon, Darrang, whose headquarters are at Tezpur. This is satisfactory only as far as the plains portion of the district is concerned, for the Civil Surgeon has no time to tour in the hills and can therefore have no first-hand knowledge of the diseases prevalent and the conditions existing in the hill villages. The Civil Surgeon is assisted by an Assistant Surgeon and one Sub-Assistant Surgeon at Lokra and one Sub-Assistant Surgeon at Charduar. There are Medical.

two dispensaries, one at Charduar and the other at Lokra. There are also two hospitals for in-patients—male and female—at the same places.

This district consists of *terai* and hill tracts, both sparsely populated. The *terai* is unhealthy like all other tracts lying under the hills in Assam. Fever is prevalent and *kala azar* has appeared. The hill tracts are free from fever, although many cases occur of fever contracted in the plains. From time to time there are outbreaks of small-pox. Cholera is very rare. Influenza has remained in the hills since the outbreak of 1919, though it has assumed a milder form. On the whole, compared with other parts of Assam, the district is healthy, as is shewn by the 5th Assam Rifles being the healthiest of the 5 Battalions stationed in the different hill districts of Assam. In the hills infant mortality accounts for the greater number of deaths. Amongst the Akas consumption caused chiefly by the insufficient ventilation of their houses is distressingly common.

Vital statistics.

Vital statistics are not reported. The birth-rate except amongst the Akas and plains Daflas is higher than the death-rate and the population is on the increase; the increase would be very large but for the heavy infant mortality. The general health of the plains people is good, except amongst the Daflas. These are all men who have left the hardships and hazards of the hills and settled in the plains where they lead a peaceful and more luxurious life. They are not used to the climate and malaria makes great ravages amongst them.

Epidemics and prevailing diseases.

Small-pox is not endemic in the hills but outbreaks occur from time to time caused by infection from the plains, these outbreaks, apart from the deaths due to them, cause much trouble, for whenever a hill village contracts the disease it invariably accuses another village nearer to the plains, of bringing in the disease and, that village is promptly raided. This leads to retaliation and often the casualties arising from these raids are more numerous than the deaths caused by the small-pox.

Malaria is naturally very prevalent in all the plains villages, as they are all situated in the unhealthy low-lying *terai*. In the hills malaria is not common, such cases as occur being contracted by persons who have been visiting or working in the plains. The hill Dafla is much more proof against malaria than the Tibetan, Bhutanese or Momba. Goitre is very common in the hills, more especially in villages where the water-supply runs through cultivation. In villages where the water comes from a rocky spring, a common source in the Aka country, no goitre will be found.

Pneumonia is very common and is probably caused by the smoke and bad ventilation of the houses.

Diarrhœa is fairly common. Cholera outbreaks are very rare.

✓Venereal diseases are unknown at present amongst the hill Akas and Daflas, but a few cases have occurred amongst the plains Daflas. With the Tibetans and Mombas, who are next-door neighbours, venereal disease of all descriptions is very common.

Kala azar is reported to be on the increase amongst the plains population. So far it is almost entirely confined to the Assamese and Kacharis. Cases are being sought out and treated and all head men have strict orders to report cases.

Education.

There is only one State Lower Primary School. It is located at Charduar, the headquarters station of the Political Officer. After the school was opened, a small number of Aka and Dafla boys attended the school, but they had to leave it as the climate of the plains did not suit them. The Akas are very anxious to have a Lower Primary School in their village.

The Daflas have not shown any interest in the education of their children.

There are two other more schools not under the control of the Education Department. One is maintained partly by subscriptions from villagers and partly by donations from the American Baptist Mission. No text-books are used here, the children being taught to read and write only. The other school is maintained by the 5th Assam Rifles to educate the children of the men of the Battalion. It is maintained from Battalion Funds and is not under the control of the Education Department.

STATEMENT B.

List of Post Offices—Lokra.*

* Combined Post and Telegraph Office.

STATEMENT C.

List of the most important Trading places.

Mauza.	Name of place.	Number of permanent shops.
1	2	3
Balipara Frontier Tract	Lokra ...	1
	Chardaur ...	1

STATEMENT D.

List of Markets.

Name of place at which market held.	Days of week when held.
1	2
Lokra	On all days throughout the year.
Doimara	On all days in the cold weather.
Amratulla	

TABLE I.

RAINFALL.

Average rainfall in inches (for 29 years).

Months.	Balipara.
1	2
January	0·68
February	1·45
March	2·48
April	6·26
May	10·82
June	16·35
July	20·32
August	15·21
September	13·92
October	6·53
November	1·62
December	0·46
Annual	96·10

TABLE II.

Distribution of Population.

District.	Population in 1921.	Population in 1911.	Difference.	Area in square miles.	Population per square mile in 1921.	Number of persons censused in tea gardens in 1921.
1	2	3	4	5	6	7
Balipara Frontier Tract.	3,819	863	+2,956	522	7	689

TABLE III.

General Statistics of Population.

Particulars.	District.		
	Persons.	Males.	Females.
1	2	3	4
Population—			
1921	3,819	2,586	1,233
1911	863	...	...
Variation—			
1911—1921	+2,956	...	...
Religion—			
Total Hindus	2,739	2,005	734
Animists	849	447	402
Muhammadans	26	21	5
Total Christians	96	56	40
(*i*) Anglican Communion... ...	6	5	1
(*ii*) Baptist	78	43	35
(*iii*) Presbyterian	...	...	...
(*iv*) Roman Catholic	7	5	2
Other Religions	18	4	14

TABLE III—*concld.*

General Statistics of Population.

Particulars.	District.		
	Persons.	Males.	Females.
1	2	3	4
Civil condition—			
Unmarried	1,692	1,135	557
Married	1,950	1,351	599
Widowed	177	100	77
Literacy—			
Literate	584	564	20
Literate in English	34	32	2
Illiterate	3,235	2,022	1,213
Languages spoken—			
Assamese	613	437	176
Bengali	62	47	15
Dafla	208	110	98
Garo	146	77	69
Khamti	101	49	52
Mikir	136	74	62
Miri	456	246	210
Hindi	80	55	25
Mundari	206	100	106
Naipali	1,268	1,059	209
Oriya	281	140	141
Santali	80	63	17
Telegu	72	37	35

TABLE IV.

Birth place, race, caste and occupation.

Particulars.	Persons.	Males.	Females.
1	2	3	4
Birth place—			
Born in the district	979	536	443
Ditto other parts of province ...	981	624	357
Ditto Bengal	90	71	19
Ditto Bihar and Orissa	609	344	265
Ditto Central Provinces and Berar ...	3	...	3
Ditto Madras (including Laccadives)	18	12	6
Ditto United Provinces	19	14	5
Ditto Nepal	1,028	936	92
Ditto elsewhere	92	49	43
Race and caste—			
Bhumij	20	9	11
Brahman	45	31	14
Dafla	203	110	93
Dom	66	34	32
Garo	98	61	37
Kachari	176	113	63
Khamti	102	50	52
Khasia	35	20	15
Koch	194	107	87
Mech	67	57	10
Mikir	140	78	62
Miri	455	245	210

TABLE IV—*concld.*

Particulars.	Persons.	Males.	Fema
1	2	3	4
Race and caste—			
Munda	59	33	26
Oraon	111	51	60
Rabha	20	14	6
Rajbansi	64	63	1
Rajput (Chhattri)	154	126	28
Santal	61	54	7
Tanti	175	94	81
Musalman (unspecified)	26	21	5
Occupation—			
Workers	2,799	2,192	607
Dependents	1,020	394	626
Total supported—			
Landlords	...	...	...
Ordinary cultivators	917	567	350
On tea gardens	501	261	241
Farm servants and field labourers ...	2	1	1
General labourers	...	...	...

TABLE V.

Reserved Forests.

Name of reserves.	Area in square miles.	Situation and character of forests.
1	2	3
Khalingduar ...	27	*Mauzas.*—Bengbari and Jhaprabari, between Bhola nadi and Chumrung nadi. *Soil.*—Alluvial, with a rich and deep vegetable mould on the surface and near the rivers, gravel underneath. The following are the timber trees :—Sam, Nahor, Ajhar, Poma, Gonserai, Mekahi, Titampa, etc.

TABLE V—*concld.*

Name of reserves.	Area in square miles.	Situation and character of forests.
1	2	3
Charduar ...	182	*Mauzas.*—Balipara, Borgong and Borchola, between Mansiri nadi and Panchnoi river. *Soil.*—With alluvial deposit with sand, clay and boulders, containing Poma, Amari, Gonserai, Uriam, Nahor, etc.
Balipara ...	82	*Mauza.*—Balipara, between Mansiri nadi and Bhorelli river. The soil is alluvial in the plains and consists of mixture of clay and sand with humus of varying proportions. Near the Bhorelli, gravel and boulders occur. Predominant trees are Sâl, Ajhar, Gonserai, Sam, Poma, Uriam, Amari, Jikri, Nahor, etc,
Nawduar ...	107	*Mausas.*—Bokala and Sootea, between Bhorelli river and Giladhari nadi. *Soil.*—Alluvial in the greater part with deep vegetable mould on the surface ; low hills chiefly consist of sandstone. Principal trees are Ajhar, Amari, Koroi, Gonserai, Poma, etc.
Bishnath ...	31	*Mauza.*—Bishnath, between Giladhari nadi and Sidharujuli *Soil.*—Is alluvial with a thick layer of humus. The sub-soil consists of chiefly sand and gravel at the lower level, while on the higher level it is sandy loam with gravel or granitoid rock underneath. Forest mixed evergreen and consists of Nahor, Poma, Amari, Dwang, Sam, Khokan, Gonserai and Simul.
Behali ...	52	*Mauza.*—Behali, between Borgong river and Boroi river. *Soil.*—Consists for the most part of good dark loam of a considerable depth, along the Borgong and Boroi rivers. The soil is of a light alluvial character, Nahor, Khair, Khokan, Gomari, Amari, Simul, Ajhar, Uriam are to be found.
Gohpur ...	52	*Mausa.*—Gohpur between Balijan and Mornoi river. *Soil.*—Is alluvial and has rich vegetable mould on the surface. The sub-soil consists of sandy loam with sand and gravel underneath. The crop consists of Nahor, Amari, Gonserai, Khokan, Uriam and Simul. There are also a few Sâl near Dubia.

TABLE

Statement showing outturn of Timber,

Details.	1913-14.	1914-15.	1915-16.	1916-17.	1917-18.	1918-19.	1919-20.	1920-21.
1	2	3	4	5	6	7	8	9
Reserved Forests :—Khalingduar, Charduar, Balipara, Nawduar, Bishnath, Behali and Gohpur—								
Area in square miles ...	333	333	380	380	535	535	534	534
Outturn (Government and purchasers only)—								
Timber ... C. ft.	35,660	46,840	22,464	48,231	46,902	50,077	61,710	66,612
Fuel ... "	77,492	92,802	115,634	101,808	47,734	54,510	69,804	40,261
Cane ... Rs.	967	1,000	229	561	559	789	1,259	1,192
Elephants ... "	Nil	Nil	Nil	Nil	Nil	Nil	Nil	Nil
Elephant tusks "	Nil	Nil	Nil	2	Nil	Nil	185	496
Thatch ... "	253	252	344	286	237	295	400	78
Unclassed State Forests :—Disforested areas and Political Unclassed State Forests—								
Area in square miles ...	Nil	Nil	Nil	Nil	Nil	Nil	46	46
Outturn (Government and Purchasers only)—								
Timber ... C.ft.	Nil	Nil	Nil	Nil	Nil	Nil	608	500
Fuel ... "	Nil	Nil	Nil	Nil	Nil	Nil	Nil	Nil
Cane ... Rs.	Nil	Nil	Nil	Nil	Nil	Nil	Nil	Nil
Elephants ... "	Nil	Nil	Nil	Nil	Nil	Nil	Nil	Nil
Thatch ... "	Nil	Nil	Nil	Nil	Nil	Nil	24	Nil
Forest Receipts... "	8,425	22,392	6,367	11,352	14,684	14,941	20,886	17,376
Expenditure ... "	15,206	36,838	3,234	4,161	4,301	2,972	5,606	12,972
Surplus or deficit "	—6,781	—15,446	3,133	7,191	10,383	11,969	15,280	4,404

VI.

Fuel and value of Minor Forest Produce.

1921-22	1922-23.	1923-24.	1924-25.	1925-26.	1926-27.	1927-28.	1928-29	1929-30.	1930-31.	1931-32.
10	11	12	13	14	15	16	17	18	19	20
534	531	533	533							
111,480	138,390	99,748	122,257							
60,324	122,870	112,082	191,111							
1,190	631	605	1,204							
2,410	24,100	22,000	25,440							
Nil	Nil	630	1,103							
523	543	258	794							
46	46	46	46							
3,150	9,070	14,148	6,149							
Nil	Nil	2,000	2,560							
Nil	Nil	Nil	Nil							
Nil	Nil	Nil	Nil							
Nil	Nil	221	Nil							
30,612	51,233	47.878	83,541							
28,059	39,863	23,215	27,209							
2,553	11,370	24,663	55,332							

TABLE VII.

Prices of food staples in seers obtainable per rupee at Lokra.

—		Common rice.	Salt.	Matikalai.
1		2	3	4
1915	2nd week of February ...	8	8	8
	2nd week of August	8	9	9
1916	2nd week of February ...	8	11	9
	2nd week of August	7	8	9
1917	2nd week of February ...	8	8	8
	2nd week of August	7	7	6
1918	2nd week of February ...	9	8	8
	2nd week of August	6	7	6
1919	2nd week of February ..	5	9	6
	2nd week of August	4½	8	5½
1920	2nd week of February ...	4⅓	8	6¼
	2nd week of August	4¼	7	6
1921	2nd week of February ...	6⅓	9	8
	2nd week of August	6	8	7
1922	2nd week of February ...	8	9	8
	2nd week of August	6¼	8	6⅓
1923	2nd week of February ...	...	...	...
	2nd week of August	...	...	...
1924	2nd week of February ...	...	...	...
	2nd week of August	...	...	...
1925	2nd week of February ...	...	...	...
	2nd week of August	...	...	...

TABLE VII—*concld.*

—	Common rice.	Salt.	*Matikalai.*
1	2	3	4
1926 { 2nd week of February ...	...	...	...
1926 { 2nd week of August	...	...	...
1927 { 2nd week of February ...	...	...	...
1927 { 2nd week of August	...	...	...
1928 { 2nd week of February ...	...	...	...
1928 { 2nd week of August	...	...	...
1929 { 2nd week of February ...	...	...	...
1929 { 2nd week of August	...	...	...
1930 { 2nd week of February ...	...	...	...
1930 { 2nd week of August	...	...	...
1931 { 2nd week of February ...	...	...	...
1931 { 2nd week of August	...	...	...
1932 { 2nd week of February ...	...	...	...
1932 { 2nd week of August	...	...	...

TABLE

Statistics of Criminal

Heads of crime.	1915.		1916.		1917.	
	True.	Detected.	True.	Detected.	True.	Detected.
1	2	3	4	5	6	7
CRIMINAL JUSTICE.						
NUMBER OF CASES.						
(I) Rioting or unlawful assembly. Sections 143-153, 157, 158, and 159.	...	...	...	...	...	...
(II) Other offences against the State, public tranquility, etc.	—	..	1	1	2	2
(III) Murder, attempt at murder and culpable homicide. Sections 302-304, 307, 308 and 396.	...	..	1	1	...	...
(IV) Grievous hurt and hurt by dangerous weapon. Sections 324-326, 329, 331, 333 and 335.	...	...	1	1	...	...
(V) Serious criminal force. Sections 353, 354, 356 and 357.	...	...	...	...	...	...
(VI) Other serious offences against the person	..	...	...	..	...	...
(VII) Dacoity. Sections 395, 397 and 398 ...	...	...	...	...	...	...
(VIII) Serious mischief, including mischief by killing, poisoning or maiming any animal. Sections 270, 281, 282, 428, 429, 430-433 and 435-440.	...	...	...	...	...	...
(IX) House breaking and serious house trespass. Sections 449-452, 454, 455 and 457-460.	...	...	1	1	1	...
(X) Wrongful restraint and confinement. Sections 341-344.	...	...	...	...	...	...
(XI) Other serious offences against the person and property or against property.	...	...	...	...	...	...
(XII) Theft. Sections 379-382	...	...	1	1	1	1
(XIII) Receiving stolen property. Sections 411 and 414.	...	...	...	...	...	...
(XIV) Lurking and criminal house-trespass. Sections 453, 460, 447 and 448.	...	...	...	...	...	...
(XV) Other minor offences against property*	9	8	5	5	3	3
Total ...	9	8	10	10	7	6
CIVIL JUSTICE.						
Suits for money and moveables	...	...	1	...	1	...
Title and other suits...	...	...	...	...	...	...
Rent suits	...	...	...	...	...	...
Total ...	...	...	1	...	1	...

* Also including offences under Special and Local Laws—8 in 1915 ;

VIII.

and Civil Justice.

1918.		1919.		1920.		1921.		1922.		1923.	
True.	Detected	True.	Detected.	True.	Detected.	True.	Detected.	True.	Detected.	True.	Detected.
8	9	10	11	12	13	14	15	16	17	18	19
...	...	...	...	...	...	.	...				
2	1	...	...	5	5	2	2				
...	...	...	...	...	...	...	...				
...	...	...	...	...	...	1	1				
...	...	..	...	...	...	...	...				
3	3	3	3	1	1	1	1				
...	...	...	...	2	2	...	...				
...	...	...	...	1	1	...	.				
...	...	...	...	...	...	...	...				
...	...	...	..	—	...	...	...				
...	...	...	...	...	...	...	...				
3	3	3	3	2	2	5	3				
...	...	...	...	...	...	...	...				
...	...	...	...	1	1	...	...				
6	8	2	2	3	3	4	4				
14	15	8	8	15	15	13	11				
2	...	...	...	1	...	...	4				
...	...	...	...	...	...	...	...				
...	...	...	...	...	...	...	...				
2	...	...	...	1	...	—	4				

5 in 1916 ; 3 in 1917 ; 6 in 1918 ; 2 in 1919 ; 8 in 1920 ; and 3 in 1921.

TABLE

Heads of crime.	1934.		1935.		1936.	
	True.	Detected.	True.	Detected.	True.	Detected.
	20	21	22	23	24	25
CRIMINAL JUSTICE.						
NUMBER OF CASES.						
(I) Rioting or unlawful assembly. Sections 143-153, 157, 158, and 159.						
(II) Other offences against the State, public tranquillity, etc.						
(III) Murder attempt at murder and culpable homicide. Sections 302-304, 307, 308 and 396.						
(IV) Grievous hurt and hurt by dangerous weapon. Sections 324-326, 329, 331, 333 and 335.						
(V) Serious criminal force. Sections 353, 354, 356 and 357.						
(VI) Other serious offences against the person						
(VII) Dacoity. Sections 395, 397 and 398 ...						
(VIII) Serious mischief, including mischief by killing, poisoning or maiming any animal. Sections 270, 281, 283, 428, 429, 430-433 and 435-440.						
(IX) House breaking and serious house trespass. Sections 449-452, 454, 455 and 457-460.						
(X) Wrongful restraint and confinement. Sections 341-344.						
(XI) Other serious offences against the person and property or against property.						
(XII) Theft. Sections 379-382						
(XIII) Receiving stolen property. Sections 411 and 414.						
(XIV) Lurking and criminal house-trespass. Sections 453, 456, 447 and 448.						
(XV) Other minor offences against property*						
Total ...						
CIVIL JUSTICE.						
Suits for money and moveables						
Title and other suits						
Rent suits						
Total ...						

* Also including offences under Special and Local Laws—3 in 1915 ;

VIII—*concld.*

1927.		1928.		1929.		1930.		1931.		1932.	
True.	Detected.	True.	Detected.	True.	Detected.	True.	Detected.	True.	Detected.	True.	Detected.
26	27	28	29	30	31	32	33	34	35	36	37

5 in 1916 ; 8 in 1917 ; 6 in 1918 ; 3 in 1919 ; 3 in 1920 ; and 3 in 1921.

TABLE

Fluctuations in

Particulars.	1913-14.	1914-15.	1915-16.	1916-17.	1917-18.	1918-19.	1919-20.	1920-21.
1	2	3	4	5	6	7	8	9
Settled area (acres)	...	...	...	2,713	2,750	3,039	2,762	2,783
Area excluded from settlement (acres) ..	...	...	...	...	...	11	300	21
Area included in settlement (acres) ...	...	...	...	...	37	300	48	23
Revenue demand (Rs.)	...	...	...	44	117	663	719	731

IX.

settled area.

1921-22.	1922-23.	1923-24.	1924-25.	1925-26.	1926-27.	1927-28.	1928-29.	1929-30.	1930-31.	1931-32.	Remarks.
10	11	12	13	14	15	16	17	18	19	20	21
2,817	3,323	3,353	...	...	...	...	...	...	...	...	Including area settled for special cultivation.
...	...	21	...	...	...	...	...	...	...	...	
34	505	52	...	...	...	...	..	...	...	...	
828	1,860	1,915	...	...	...	...	...	...	...	...	

TABLE

Finance

Principal heads.	1914-15.	1915-16.	1916-17.	1917-18.	1918-19.	1919-20.	1920-21.	1921-22.
1	2	3	4	5	6	7	8	9
		Rs.	Rs.	Rs.	Rs.	Rs.	Rs.	Rs.
Land Revenue	...	...	44	117	682	696	741	646
Local rate *	...	...	8	7	42	43	47	64
Miscellaneous Revenue: Upset sale price of Waste land.	...	...	2,688	...	...	...	...	...
Mutation Fees	...	...	...	...	18	...	...	...
Income-tax	...	...	669	808	822	807	740	2,575
Excise (opium)	...	...	2,160	1,560	1,200	1,800	1,010	408
Grazing Tax	...	...	...	315	255	160	345	600
Inner Line Pass	...	60	...	72	36	125	3	171
Pound Collections	...	...	...	270	446	360	338	298
Gun License fees	...	3	...	4	4	39	55	30
Forest Revenue †(a)	...	...	...	...	...	...	...	...

* There being no Local Fund in this district, the local

† (a) Forest Revenue realised on the settled areas in the Forest Reserves, and also for royalty accounts of the

X.

Receipts.

1922-23.	1923-24.	1924-25.	1925-26.	1926-27.	1927-28.	1928-29.	1929-30.	1930-31.	1931-32.	Remarks.
10	11	12	13	14	15	16	17	18	19	20

rate realised is credited as Revenue Receipts.
on elephant captured, and duty on forest produce, such as wax, tusk, etc., are credited.
district of Darrang.

TABLE

Land

Particulars.	1913-14.	1914-15.	1915-16.	1916-17.	1917-18.	1918-19.	1919-20.	1920-21.
1	2	3	4	5	6	7	8	9
				Acres.	Acres.	Acres.	Acres.	Acres.
Total land settled for ordinary cultivation.	...	...	...	25	62	351	94	95
Held on ordinary tenures ...	...	..	...	25	62	351	94	95
Held Revenue-free	...	...	...	...	...	...	...	...
Held at half rates	...	...	...	...	...	...	...	...
Total land settled for special cultivation.	...	...	...	2,688	2,088	2,688	2,68	2,688
Free-simple and commuted grants.	...	..	...	...	...	...	...	...
Settled on 30 years' lease ...	...	...	...	2,088	2,688	2,688	2,688	2,688
Re-settled on expiry of 30 years' lease.	...	...	...	...	...	...	...	...
Total land settled under other tenures.	...	...	...	..	...	...	...	...
Total settled area of the district	...	...	..	2,713	2,750	3,039	2,782	2,783
Total unsettled area of the district.				Unknown.				

XI.

Tenures.

1921-22.	1922-23.	1923-24.	1924-25.	1925-26.	1926-27.	1927-28.	1928-29.	1929-30.	1930-31.	1931-32.	Remarks.
10	11	12	13	14	15	16	17	18	19	20	21
Acres.	Acres.	Acres.									
129	634	665									
129	634	665									
...	...	...									
.	—	...									
2,688	2,688	2,688									
..	...	...									
2,688	2,688	2,688	...	...	...	...	...	...	...	...	The figures are the same as under land settled for special cultivation.
...	...	...									
...	...	...									
3,317	3,322	3,353									

TABLE

Education (State Lower

Particulars.	1914-15.	1915-16.	1916-17.	1917-18.	1918-19.	1919-20.	1920-21.
1	2	3	4	5	6	7	8
Middle English School—							
Number ...	...	...	...	...	...	...	...
Number of boys ...	...	...	...	...	...	...	...
Lower Primary School—							
Number ...	...	...	...	...	1	1	1
Number of boys reading in 3 upper classes.	...	...	...	...	2	1	5
Number of boys reading in lower classes.	...	...	...	...	26	26	28

XII.

Primary School).

1921-22.	1922-23.	1923-24.	1924-25.	1925-26.	1926-27.	1927-28.	1928-29.	1929-30.	1930-31.	1931-32.
9	10	11	12	13	14	15	16	17	18	19
...	...	...	...	...	...	...	...	...	...	...
...	...	...	...	...	...	...	...	...	...	...
1	1	1	1	...	...	...	...	...	...	...
8	8	7	11	...	...	...	...	...	...	...
30	20	35	22	...	...	...	...	...	...	...

TABLE XIII.

Educational Finance.

Particulars.	Number of institutions.	Expenditure on institutions maintained or aided by Public Funds in 1920-21 from: Provincial Revenue.	District or Municipal fund.	Fees.	Other sources.	Total.	Expenditure per school.
1	2	3	4	5	6	7	8
Chardnar State Lower Primary School.	1	203	...	...	...	203	...
	1	203	...	...	...	203	...

TABLE XIV.

Medical.

Particulars.	1911.	1921.
1	2	3
Number of dispensaries	...	1
Daily average number of in-door patients	...	4·78
Daily average number of out-door patients	...	15·12
Cases treated	...	3,129
Total income	...	2,734
Income from Government	...	2,734
Income from Local and Municipal funds	...	...
Subscriptions	...	...
Total expenditure	...	2,734
Expenditure on establishment ...	...	2,806

Note.—Another dispensary at Chardnar was opened from 1922.

TABLE XV.

Dispensaries.

Name of dispensary.	1914.		1915.		1916.		1917.		1918.	
	Total cost.	Cases treated.	Total cost.	Cases treated.	Total cost.	Cases treated.	Total cost.	Cases treated.	Total cost.	Cases treated.
1	2	3	4	5	6	7	8	9	10	11
ORDINARY DISPENSARY.					Rs.		Rs.		Rs.	
Lokra	...	...	...	...	1,182	1,144	1,277	1,472	1,304	2,786

Name of dispensary.	1919.		1920.		1921.		1922.		1923.	
	Total cost.	Cases treated.	Total cost.	Cases treated.	Total cost.	Cases treated.	Total cost.	Cases treated.	Total cost.	Cases treated.
	12	13	14	15	16	17	18	9	20	21
ORDINARY DISPENSARY.	Rs.		Rs.		Rs.		Rs.		Rs.	
Lokra	1,665	3,083	2,153	2,906	2,734	3,129	8,962	3,378	6,167	3,130
Chardwar	...	...	...	...	...	...	2,578	3,27	2,950	8,752

TABLE XV—*concld.*

Name of dispensary.	1924.		1925.		1926.		1927.		1928.	
	Total cost.	Cases treated.	Total cost.	Cases treated.	Total cost.	Cases treated.	Total cost.	Cases treated.	Total cost.	Cases treated.
	22	23	24	25	26	27	28	29	30	31
ORDINARY DISPENSARY.										
Lokra	4,114	2,938	4,200	3,564	4,002	3,770	...	...	...	...
Charduar	2,662	3,393	2,597	3,159	3,906	4,401	...	...	...	...

Name of dispensary.	1929.		1930.		1931.		1932.	
	Total cost.	Cases treated.	Total cost.	Cases treated.	Total cost.	Cases treated.	Total cost.	Cases treated.
	32	33	34	35	36	37	38	39
ORDINARY DISPENSARY.	...	...	...	...	...	...	...	...
Lokra	...	...	...	...	...	...	...	...

INDEX.

A

B

C

D

PAGE.

R

S

PAGE.

T

U

V

W